INFORMED CONSENT

Informed Consent

Jane Cowles

Coward, McCann & Geoghegan, Inc.
New York

Anatomical drawings courtesy of Vernon C. Kimmel.

SBN: 698-10682-2

Library of Congress Catalog Card Number: 75-10466
Library of Congress Cataloging in Publication Data

Cowles, Jane Kelliher,
Informed consent.

Bibliography: p.
Includes index.
1. Breast—Cancer. 2. Cancer patients.
3. Informed consent (Medical law) I. Title.
RC280.B8C66   616.9'94'49   75-10466

PRINTED IN THE UNITED STATES OF AMERICA

In memory of a courageous woman
My sister
SUSAN KELLIHER NORRIE

Contents

Acknowledgments

I wish to acknowledge the following institutions, staffs, and individuals who made this study possible:

I thank the Los Angeles County General Hospital and the University of Southern California Medical Center for allowing me to immerse myself totally in their clinics, wards, surgery rooms, patient discussion groups, pathology departments, lectures, tumor boards, radiation departments, medical oncology departments, and social services.

I thank my overall medical adviser, Dr. Findlay Russell, who watched over my project, provided me with laboratory space, and in particular instilled in me, through great patience and dedication, a scientific approach to all aspects of my work. I also thank the following physicians, psychologists, professional staff, and friends for their selfless, ongoing concern and availability:

Dr. Bernard Feder, who imparted balance and insight;

Dr. Henry Jenny, who gave me insight and courage to write this book;

Dr. Richard Myles, who cared;

Dr. Roger Terry, who brought the world of pathology alive for me;

Mr. Paul Saevig, who gave me literary insight;

Dr. William Glasser, who helped me remain in touch with reality;

Mr. Jacques de Spoelberch, who had faith;

Dr. Evelyen Wilkenson, who was always available;

Dr. Creighton G. Bellinger, who encouraged me;

Dr. Ralph E. Johnson, who gave of his time;

Jane Cowles

Dr. William Moss, for evaluating the manuscript;
Dr. Richard Ellerby, for proofing the final manuscript;
Mr. Henry Gonzales, who always listened;
Mr. John Oldenkamp, for his sensitive photography;
Mr. Clark Kimmel, for his brilliant illustrations;
Dr. John G. Miller, for his assistance;
Dr. Neil G. McCluskey, a great educational inspiration;
and all of the hundreds of individuals who gave selflessly of their time and knowledge.

In particular, I would like to acknowledge the Leon Mandel family, who allowed a camp to be set up in their home for ten days. I am particularly grateful to Dutch Mandel for supplying comic relief; to Avie Mandel, for reading; to Olivia Mandel, an astute critic; to Leon Mandel, who is likely one of the greatest combined writers, teachers, supporters, editors, and psychologists of all time.

Congressman Frederick W. Richmond, who understood the urgent need for this research project.

The late Mr. Peter Revson, who urged me toward excellence by his words and his example of dedication and commitment.

My late sister, Susan Kelliher Norrie, who inspired me by her example of courage in both life and death.

Los Angeles, California

Foreword

The Why of This Book

How did I come to have such strong feelings about breast cancer? Through the years, I was aware of its existence. I knew of women who had it. They were, for the most part, friends of my mother. Other people discussed them in subdued tones with torn voices, whispering solemn observations on "how sad it was," or even worse, "I knew she would die." Breast cancer was not discussed openly. It remained the subject of hushed conversations overheard in hospital corridors, in funeral homes, and on the great American telephone. During the last several years, however, there has been a new national awareness of cancer of the breast. Several popular women's magazines published token articles suggesting that women might consider less radical avenues of cancer treatment than traditional mastectomy. The main avenue, however, still conceded at least one breast to the surgeon's knife.

These articles held my interest, but I had no personal involvement until two years ago. A person who is extremely close to me dared to speak up. With breast cancer diagnosed, she dared to refuse the traditional surgical method of treatment and managed to avoid the loss of a breast. Even though she chose acceptable medical options—she fought an ocean of medical experts to preserve a breast that was part of her body. She said that she valued the

11

quality of life, which meant life with two breasts—and most doctors simply did not know what she was talking about. This observation of a woman's battle against insensitive physicians, and her unswerving dedication to her body as a entity impressed me deeply. I watched, listened to, and consumed her experience. Her struggle left a mark on me, and so I address this book to those thousands of breast cancer patients in the thousand nameless hospitals throughout the country who were never given sufficient preparation or information during their ordeals, the many women who never knew they *had a right of choice,* a right of self-determination—a human right, more basic than any of our rights under the Constitution.

It is essential to grasp the concept that women can be trusted to make the right decisions about their bodies, just as long as they have the right information. However, this cannot come about unless women are properly examined, educated, and informed, something many physicians fail to do. Women must force their doctors to do so, armed with education, strength, and determination, for it is unlikely these urgent changes will come from the medical profession quickly enough. Women must help physicians to learn about the dignity of a woman's body. Women must help physicians to be fully aware that a true healer heals not only the body, but the mind and the spirit as well.

The two composite case histories presented in this book are bound together by the diagnosis of breast cancer. Their similarity ends there. Meg Land and Olivia Newman could be two of the 90,000 cases of diagnosed breast cancer in the United States in 1975.

The basis for obtaining knowledge about breast examination and breast-cancer treatment is information. Simply stated, the patient must be informed. In 1975 the Health, Education and Welfare Department redefined "informed consent." Doctors are bound—morally and by law—to inform their patients of any procedure that might put the patient "at risk." HEW reported that "an individual is considered 'at risk' if she may be exposed to the possibility of harm—physical, psychological, sociological, or other as a consequence of treatment."

They have defined informed consent as follows:

The knowing consent of an individual or her legally authorized representative, so situated as to be able to exercise free power of choice without undue inducement or any element of force, fraud, deceit, duress, or other form of constraint or coercion. The basic elements of information necessary to such consent include:

1. A fair explanation of the procedure to be followed, and their purposes, including identification of any procedures which are experimental

2. A description of any attendant discomfort and risks reasonably to be expected

3. A description of any benefits reasonably to be expected

4. Disclosure of any appropriate alternative procedures that might be advantageous for the subject

5. An offer to answer any inquiries concerning procedures

6. An instruction that the person is free to withdraw his consent and to discontinue participation in the project or activity at any time without prejudice to the subject.

The above should be common knowledge to individuals involved in health care. It is also imperative for them to remember that the patient is a *total person* and should be treated as such. Illness is a frightening, psychologically disturbing experience. While the patient has the right to be fully informed (unless otherwise medically or psychologically contraindicated), that informing must be handled delicately and should not be left to nurses or others.

Informed consent is in hot debate across the nation today. The American Civil Liberties Union has produced an excellent book, *The Rights of Hospital Patients,* covering all aspects of the issue. Many patients do not know they have any rights while in a clinic, doctor's office, or hospital. But that is simply not true. We all know that the standard procedure for the biopsy of a breast lump is admission to the hospital with mastectomy possible. Meg Land's is such a case. While reading about Meg Land, decide for yourself if she experienced a frank and full discussion of the alternatives available, their risks, and the probabilities of success—the essential prelude to giving a truly informed consent.

Informed Consent

Author's note

Studies reporting the results of various forms of cancer treatments have been omitted from this book.

No one cancer treatment has yet been indicated as the "proper" therapy, and no long discussions of drug therapy have been included.

The purpose of *Informed Consent* is to disclose relevant and simple information concerning the premalignant and postmalignant breast state. Armed with an outline of this book, it is hoped that women can participate as fully as possible in the exercise of control over their own bodies.

J.K.C.

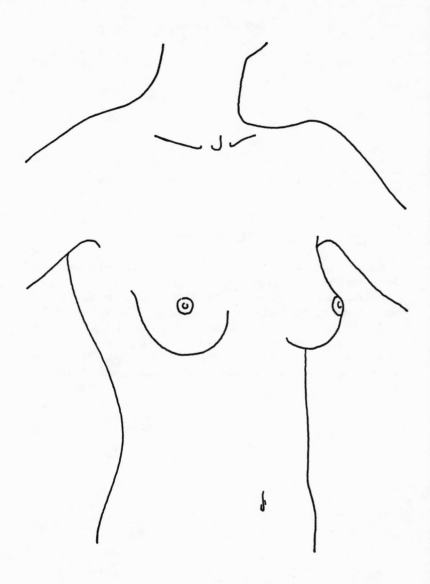

The normal breast

ONE
Meg Land

Meg Land is forty-two. She has naturally curly, silver-streaked black hair, brown eyes, a small turned-up nose, and perfect teeth. It is difficult to know Meg. She has a guarded personality. She laughs a little too often, a little too hard. Meg is married to Barry Land, a tall, blond, ruggedly handsome executive. They live in a comfortable home on the outskirts of Beverly Hills with their four children, two boys and two girls, all under fifteen. Meg and Barry have never had a relationship you could call warm and open. Barry has his own life—and that life is his work. Meg is kept busy with her children, her charities, and Barry's social and work demands. Their friends and neighbors see them as a "good couple."

Meg has always considered herself healthy and full of vitality. She is well aware of some aspects of breast cancer, and a number of her friends have had radical mastectomies. Since Meg spends a good deal of time at home, she has read in the popular magazines those dozens and dozens of articles on breast cancer. She was an avid sympathizer when Happy Rockefeller and Betty Ford went through their ordeals. She has even been a neighborhood campaigner for the American Cancer Society. Meg is convinced she looks after her health and makes it a practice to visit her respected gynecologist once a year for a Pap smear. But Meg—despite her knowledge of breast cancer and participation in fund raising— does not now examine, nor has she ever examined, her own breasts. And neither has her physician.

In this sense, Meg is typical. In a 1974 Gallup Poll, more than three-fourths of the women surveyed did not have a physician who examined their breasts at every visit. Even among women who see a gynecologist for regular checkups, only 50 percent say their breasts are examined routinely. With her reading and cancer charity work, Meg should be more enlightened—more aware of breast cancer than others—but she is not.

Despite the massive public education campaign of last year, both Meg and her physician have ignored the practice of regular breast examination. Meg's family doctor has never had her referred to a radiologist for X rays of the breast, called screening mammograms*, or xerograms, even though, being over forty, Meg falls into the higher risk category of being a cancer candidate. Meg is considered high risk for the following reasons: She is over forty. She began menstruating at ten. She did not have any children until she was twenty-five. She is in a high socioeconomic bracket, and her mother had cancer of the breast. Had the doctor referred her, or had Meg been informed of the above modes of detection, it might have been possible to detect any unusual changes in her left breast.

One evening, after dinner, Meg was luxuriating in the bathtub. As she soaped herself around her breasts, she felt something in her left breast, slightly above the nipple, that seemed hard and raised. She casually returned her fingers to her breast to see if it was her imagination. It was not. There was a lump in her breast. She lay very still in the water, feeling the lump over and over. She rinsed off, dried herself, and moved closer to the mirror to see if it was visible. It was not, but she could still feel it with her fingers. After the surprise of discovering the lump, Meg's immediate feeling was anxiety. Her mind teemed with a million questions as she methodically dressed and joined her husband in the living room. Besides

*See note, page 66.

the anxiety, she was now experiencing fear—hollow and chilling. Reluctantly Meg acknowledged to herself that the lump was there and that she must do something about. But where could she start?

Meg excused herself and went to bed early. There in the darkened room, she lay quietly, tears running down her cheeks. It was that first night that set Meg Land up for the four-month ordeal that would follow. She had always been figure-proud, even after having her four children. As she wept, the thought of what the lump could mean rushed through her mind. She explored it all—cancer, losing a breast, losing her life. Meg put herself through the whole experience—real and unreal—the trap of the imagination working overtime, the uninformed imagination conjuring devils and finding smoke where there was no fire.

The next day she awoke with a pounding headache. Throughout the long hours, the previous evening's discovery replayed in her mind. She stopped her task of salad making and looked out the window. What should she do? Available information tells us she could react in many different ways.

A noted breast specialist in Los Angeles says that this moment of breast lump discovery, and the woman's realization that it might be cancer, may well be one of the most significant and introspective of a woman's life. There is a sudden flashback into her past and forward into the future—her family, her husband, her children . . . the very real possibility of her death . . . how she will live out the rest of her days, *if* she can handle it at all. It makes a numbing and terrifying montage.

The detection of a lump and the possibility of cancer is a lonely experience. No matter how many articles Meg has read, or television programs she has seen, nothing can possibly begin to calm or reassure her. She is in a state of emotional anguish—sometimes paralysis.

How Meg will deal with this crisis of detection and terror cannot be precisely predicted. Foreshadowings of her reaction might be discovered in the way she has solved past crises in her life. Yet, *this* experience—and you must remember that Meg has no know-

ledge of whether the lump is cancer or not—is totally unlike anything else that has ever happened to her.

Her level of anxiety is the factor that probably results in Meg's
delay in talking about the lump—much less in going to her doctor
to have it examined. A study has shown that Meg's delay can be
attributed to a kind of breakdown in her processing of information
and the present knowledge she may already have. In other words,
although she has all the information she needs to take some sort
of rational action—she knows she has a breast lump and she knows
it could be cancer—somehow she just can't do anything about it
for the moment. This short-circuiting can take many forms. Meg
may avoid the lump—may simply disregard its existence. She may
suppress the knowledge that it is present and dismiss it entirely.
Or she may take the fatalistic approach—"If it is cancer, that's
just my destiny"—another form of mental escape. Meg is in a
crisis state. Some psychologists have postulated an average time
of four to six weeks before a woman can sufficiently marshal her
weakened emotional resources to call her doctor. Even educated
women have been known to live in a crisis state for five years or
more—living with the lump, before they seek medical attention.
Meg is living with her lump.

It is unforgivable that Meg's breasts have never been properly
examined by her doctor on a regular basis, and it is unbelievable
that she has never practiced breast self-examination. It is unfortunate that she never used any early modes of detection such as
xerography. It might have been possible earlier to detect Meg's
now easy-to-feel breast lump.

It has been amply shown by data that the early clinical detection
of a lump in a woman's breast is the first step in the right direction. But the doctor's or woman's discovery of a one-centimeter
lump (about the size of a pea) finds her with a lump that is biologically already advanced. Meg Land's one-centimeter lump in the
left breast contains over a million cells and has roughly undergone
thirty doublings since it first became the "errant" cell. It could
have been present in Meg's breast for over seven years. There are

no laws; it could have been present for a shorter time. Even though Meg's lump is small, if it is cancer, the disease could have had time to spread through her body.

Since clinically the smallest lump a qualified doctor can feel is about one centimeter—less than one quarter inch—sophisticated methods are needed to detect lumps smaller than a centimeter. Meg's only earlier answer would have been found in the medical area called "subclinical diagnosis." This simply means making use of medical tools which have the eyes a doctor cannot have. X rays of her breast called mammograms and xerograms are precious detectors in the hands of qualified radiologists and skilled technicians. Their use is in a relentless search for the tiny breast cancer . . . hidden unsuspected, possibly intact without spread.

The smaller the lump when detected and treated the higher the survival rate, and therefore, the longer the lifespan.

In Meg's case, three points can already be made: One, both the physician and Meg herself should have regularly examined her breasts. Two, if Meg's physician had made it a practice to examine her breasts on a regular basis, he might have been suspicious earlier and used mammography or xerography as a valuable contribution to his assessment of the overall situation. Three, if he had felt the lump or change in Meg's breast, or if she had been taught to examine her breasts regularly and *she* had felt the change, mammography or xerography could have been used to confirm the diagnosis at the earliest possible stage.

Also, since Meg now has a lump in her left breast, a mammogram or xerogram should be performed before any biopsy. The rationale behind this is clear. After a biopsy there will be remaining scar tissue and there will have been a pictorial record of what Meg's breast looked like before the biopsy that can be compared to mammography or xerography examinations done at a later date.

Some physicians concerned with the problems of inadequate breast examination attribute the ambivalence and resultant inaction to a combination of factors. One problem is the doctor's time. It takes time to perform a proper breast examination. It is not just a matter of spending a few minutes to feel the breast here and there. A thorough examination can often take substantially more than fifteen minutes. Another problem is that a breast examination takes practice on the part of the physician. Also there may often be an underlying sense of some embarrassment between the doctor and patient that makes the doctor hesitant to examine a woman's breast thoroughly or to discuss breast self-examination with her. Finally, and importantly, breast self-examination has never been part of the past educational health programs in this country.

If Meg had known how to examine her breasts properly each month, she would have been twelve times more familiar with her own particular lumps and bumps than a physician who saw her just once a year. In the same 1974 Gallup Poll 75 percent of the women questioned did not perform breast self-examination. The poll also showed that the women most likely to examine themselves regularly were those who had been taught the procedure by a physician. Unfortunately, fewer than one-fourth of the women surveyed had received any personal direction from their physician.

Let us suppose that Meg has sadly buried the discovery of the lump in her daily activities—the house, the children, guests from out of town, her involvement in various business and social engagements. Sometimes Meg aches all over. But each day, she is able to push the thought of the lump and seeing the doctor further from her mind. She has made her decision. The "when" of seeing her doctor entailed "when" she finally got around to it. She didn't know—or she didn't or wouldn't understand—that the longer she waited, the worse the lump was getting. The longer she waited, the more she became a stranger in her own home. The communication between her and Barry was more distant. Sadly, Barry was influenced by his wife's attitude. They became two people living in the same house, yet apart. Roommates, bedmates—the happenstance parents of four children. Meg has mechanically gotten her children off to school and cared for the house. For months she has been aware of the lump. It has not gone away. It has even grown. She and her husband have never had an easy communication, or been able to express their feelings openly. Discussion of unpleasant aspects of life—especially weakness or sickness—has always been avoided by her husband. The Land family has built a series of ritual habits and interrelationships over the years that confront Meg in this desperate hour of need to communicate—and prevent her from doing it. Out of habit Meg and Barry just don't talk about things like this. The result is an angry Meg—depressed, yet with a poignant urge to be dependent. She cannot ask her husband and family to hear or understand her anger, much less to allow her to be a dependent person . . . though she is in desperate need of an abundance of love, understanding, and acceptance.

This painful pattern is again one familiar to psychologists. Patients are often supported in their behavior by a family structure that has existed and has been reinforced for years. Only the participants can really know what goes on inside a marriage, family, or household. It is easy enough to keep up a front.

It has taken four months, but finally Meg decides to call her doctor. The receptionist asks what the problem is. It is with great difficulty that Meg is able to say first that she has located a lump in her breast. It is even more awkward to tell the impersonal voice on the other end of the phone that she has known about it for four months. All the fears which, although suppressed, have been growing focus on the moment when Meg prepares to see her doctor. What if it is cancer? The word sends her mind hurtling into terror. What if she has to have a mastectomy? Again she closes her mind.

In the doctor's waiting room, Meg glances at her watch, calming herself with the idea that it is likely to be nothing major . . . probably just a small cyst. Meg has made the appointment secretly. Barry does not even know she is there. When she is called into the examaning room, Meg manages a small, tight smile as she is greeted by her doctor,

As Meg's tall, gray-haired, bow-tied doctor examines her breasts, her mind drifts away. The doctor examines both breasts, then tells her she can get dressed and asks her to join him in his office. For long, anxious minutes Meg sits awaiting her doctor. When he joins her, he is brief. "Meg, I am suspicious of this lump and I would like to refer you to a general surgeon, a good man. I think you should have a biopsy."

The doctor says nothing to unburden Meg or alleviate her anxiety. Somehow she finds herself in the reception room again, listening to the starched receptionist making an appointment with a doctor she does not know. Her fears have not been allayed. The lump is ominously and fearfully still present.

That evening, the children having already been fed, Barry and Meg have dinner alone. Barry is in his usual mood after a few drinks, involved in rambling anecdotes about his corporate woes. Meg wants to tell him what happened that morning in the doctor's office. Finally she says, "Barry, I discovered a lump in my breast. I saw the doctor about it today." Barry lifts his glass of wine and takes a slow sip. He looks across the table at his wife. "Well, what are they going to do about it?" Meg explains she has been referred to a general surgeon to have her breast examined for a possible biopsy, Barry asks if the surgeon is "a good man." Meg replies that she doesn't know, but that he comes highly recommended. The possible opening of the complexities of Meg's feelings about the lump in her breast is swiftly evaded as Barry moves his chair away from the table and announces he is going to the den to deal with his briefcase. Meg sits at the head of the table, alone, preoccupied, turning the stem of her wineglass in circles.

The next day, Thursday, Meg finds herself filling out the standard forms that receptionists at all doctors' offices require. Once again she is invited into the examining room, again undressed, again examined, and again asked to join the doctor in his office. His recommendation is also brief. "Mrs. Land, I feel that this lump should be taken out at once. Fortunately I have an opening in my operating-room schedule tomorrow morning and my nurse has spoken with the hospital. They can take you in late this afternoon.

26

Does that fit in with your schedule?" He continues, "You know, most of these things are minor, most of them are benign. I'm sure you'll have nothing to worry about. But you do know that breast cancer is nothing to fool around with. . . . While you are in surgery, if this lump proves to be cancer, I will have to remove your breast."

The surgeon continues talking, but Meg hears only bits and pieces of what he is saying. Her mind and emotions have only absorbed a few words.

As one of the more prominent breast specialists in the country points out, despite assurances that the lump will probably be benign, 80 percent of all women "feel" it will be cancerous. Meg is one of them. She has tuned out the surgeon's words completely now and is only aware of a bespectacled, balding, white-coated stranger speaking at her soundlessly as though someone had turned off the television voice-over.

So Meg agrees. The sooner the biopsy, the better. Yes, she will check into the hospital that day around four. She leaves the surgeon's office feeling totally alone and drained. When she gets home, she calls Barry at work to tell him she will be having a biopsy the next morning, Friday. All this has been arranged without discussion between man and wife, surgeon and couple. Barry is left slightly concerned but thinks the situation minor. Still, he feels somehow anxious. He buzzes his secretary and lights a cigarette. "I guess you'll have to cancel my meeting tomorrow morning. Mrs. Land will be going to the hospital." He sits back in his leather chair, unable to concentrate on a proposal he was drafting. Meg can't reveal her fears to Barry now; the habit of silence has been too long entrenched. There is no communication between them.

Meg has placed herself in the surgeon's hands, and she has no idea what the outcome will be . . . nor is she the least bit prepared should the biopsy reveal the presence of cancer. She is prepared only to be terrified, she is not equipped to handle the biopsy or its possible consequences.

That night, lying in a strange hospital bed, Meg is confused and numb. Drugged by her own emotionally altered body chemistry, she is anxious to the point of weariness. Meg tries desperately to remember some of the things the surgeon said to her during their brief encounter, but she cannot. The entire event is cloudy and has moved by her too quickly. Meg is reaching for some questions she would like to ask the surgeon, but when he sweeps into her room, they are forgotten. A nurse is with him, and his words scythe again into her consciousness: "If it is cancer, I will have to remove your breast."

Meg's mind stumbles over what the surgeon has said. She is distracted by his talk of advanced medicine today, medical jargon and the now familiar "nothing to worry about." An operating permit to protect the hospital and physician is introduced, briefly read, and signed by Meg. It ensures among other things that, if cancer is found, the surgeon is legally cleared to go ahead and perform whatever operation "he thinks is necessary." This signed release has now delivered the destiny of Meg Land's breast, body, and future to the surgeon, who is suddenly gone. The hospital door hisses shut. Meg's thoughts are interrupted by a nurse who is taking blood samples to type and cross-match her blood with four reserve pints, in case it should be needed in surgery the next morning. The interruptions continue. An anesthesiologist is her next visitor. He tells her she will be given a general anesthesia for a minor biopsy.

Meg is about to have what is known as a "one-stage procedure." There are several major problems with this technique. One is the administration of the general anesthesia. As S. O. Schwartz's book, *Principles of Surgery,* aptly puts it: "No presently available anesthetic agent or technique is ideal. Because no anesthetic agent is perfect, each anesthesia represents a physiologic and pharmacologic trespass and inherently entails a certain risk. In an individual case the risk may be greater or smaller, but it cannot be eliminated." Schwartz points out that anesthetic risk, in terms of death rates, runs a consistent 1 in 1,600. This includes all types of anesthesia, from the most minor to the most major. This is a serious public health problem in itself. There are 450,000 breast biopsies performed each year in the United States. Meg is taking a small but recognizable risk by undergoing a minor procedure biopsy this way. She is risking possible overdosage, cardiac arrest, respiratory depression, or other difficulties.

Thus, since a breast biopsy yields a 75- to 78-percent negative pathology—a benign (noncancerous) result—it is questionable whether Meg should be subjected to a general anesthesia. Even if her doctor adheres to the older theory of operating at once if the diagnosis should be cancer, a properly premedicated Meg could easily go on to a general anesthesia if needed. Thus the argument of giving the patient two general anesthesias is countered. The alternative is to have Meg premedicated and semiawake for the biopsy. This is done by a Novocain-like drug injected into her breast so that the surgeon can sample the tissue for the pathology diagnosis. This is known as "a two-stage procedure," or a "local biopsy."

This brings up the issue of separating the biopsy and the possible treatment, if cancer is diagnosed. Meg is about to endure the one-stage procedure, but being subjected to a general anesthetic is not the only problem (although some surgeons argue that, if the lump is deep or the patient does not want to be semiawake for the minor biopsy, a general anesthetic should be given). Sadly, if Meg does have cancer of the breast, and her surgeon rushes into removing her breast, she will not have had a complete check via body scans and blood tests to see if the cancer has moved beyond her breast and into her body. These tests are known as a "metastatic workup."

Meg's is an all-too-frequent scenario. A woman has a diagnosed breast cancer, and her surgeon removes her breast, only to discover shortly after the physically and emotionally deforming operation that the woman had widespread cancer. The big operation would not have cured the cancer, and she has needlessly suffered the complete loss of a breast.

As A. S. Earle points out, "There are few procedures that are so stereotyped that they do not deserve reevaluation, including even the time-honored approach to the surgical treatment of carcinoma of the breast. Contrary to common belief, immediate mastectomy after a positive biopsy does not ensure a higher survival rate." A major hospital operating room is being tied up for Meg's minor procedure. A twenty-minute biopsy done this way results in an average hospital stay of 2.4 days with an average cost of $479, not including the surgeon's fees. And the emotional cost to Meg Land cannot be estimated. *She may or may not awaken with a breast, and she has not been and will not be a part of that decision.* For Meg, the antiseptic confusion and blur moves faster now as her questions and doubts are lost to sleeping pills and injections. Barry has come late to the hospital and brings flowers. Once again they say very little, and as Barry leans down to kiss her on the forehead, he pats Meg's hand and assures her everything will be fine.

Meg's awakening the next morning is jangled, as she is instructed to shower with a special soap and put on a hospital gown with the opening in the front. The floor nurse gives her an injection in the hip. Her last memory before surgery is of her body bumping slightly as the rubber wheels deliver her to the operating room. Barry once again briefly encounters his wife as she leaves for the operating room. He sits in room 608, noting the bland green walls, the spareness of the room, and the absence of his wife. He wishes he had gotten to the hospital earlier to spend a little more time with Meg.

Once into the operating room, Meg is transferred onto the operating table. The entire staff is masked and gowned in green. The nurses are busy. Meg's gown is opened to expose her chest. One nurse with gloved hands and sterile forceps is methodically swabbing Meg's chest with a brown liquid soap. Another drapes her body with many sterile green cloths and sheets that are clipped together. Finally, the only remaining identification of Meg Land is the left breast where the surgeon will perform the biopsy. A green cloth screen has been placed between Meg's face and the breast. Meg's right arm, opposite the breast to be biopsied, is outstretched from her side as the anesthesia is administered. The anesthesiologist is sitting at Meg's head. He is attempting to accomplish what is known as "securing an airway." This entails inserting lubricated tubes into her throat. In the event that Meg should stop voluntary breathing during the biopsy, the tube in her throat can be used to keep her alive by using a respirator to fill her lungs with air a few times each minute. Since she is under general anesthesia, her heart is being monitored. Bottle of intravenous fluid are hung from the nearby chrome stand should the biopsy prove the presence of cancer.

The surgeon enters the room, having completed an earlier gallbladder removal, one of the four operations he will perform today. With him is one of the hospital's rotating surgical interns. The surgeon asks for Meg's chart to refamiliarize himself with what he is about to do. Both the senior and junior surgeons scrub, gown, and glove themselves and now are considered "sterile." The surgeon moves to Meg's left side, feels for the lump in her left breast, and asks the intern to do the same. He is handed a scalpel from the sterile tray. He makes an incision over the lump. The surgeon asks a nurse to adjust the light. An instrument known as an electrocoagulator is used to stop the bleeding from the incision by burning the tissue. It makes a hissing sound as the surgeon burns one small blood vessel after another. The surgical nurse hands the surgeon scissors, which he uses to spread the incision wider. The intern assists the surgeon by using gauze pads called sponges to dab blood out of the incision in order to keep the visual field of the incision as clear as possible. The intern is now in charge of the coagulator. The surgeon inserts his finger into the incision. He locates the lump and clamps hold of the two sides of the suspicious tissue with another instrument that clips the tissue with a sharp sound. A section of the tissue is cut away, lifted out, examined by the surgeons, and placed in sterile towels the nurse is holding. She is to deliver the tissue to the pathologist for what is known as a "frozen-section diagnosis." As the surgeon sutures the incision closed, the tissue specimen is delivered to the pathologist. Meg is still asleep on the operating table, and the entire surgical staff awaits the pathologist's decision. There is a distinct air of tension in the operating room.

A Rapid Diagnosis

As Meg Land lies on a hospital operating table, the biopsy tissue has arrived downstairs at the pathology lab for the frozen-tissue examination. Even now, the surgeon is pressing the pathologist on the telephone for a diagnosis. Sometimes a report is given by a pathologist who is not entirely sure of the frozen-section diagnosis. What appeared to be cancerous at the time of the frozen diagnosis is revealed as benign when a more thorough examination is completed. *Nonetheless, a breast amputation has already been performed.*

When that happens, everyone is at fault. The surgeon is pressed for time, the pathologist may have had doubts that only a lengthy study could resolve, and the patient has put her complete faith in the physician. Nevertheless, the story illustrates the vital importance of a thorough pathology study—in this case lengthy permanent-tissue examination.

Yet, asleep under general anesthetic, Meg is not aware that two types of tissue examination techniques are used, *frozen section* and *permanent section*. The tissue specimen taken from her breast in the operating room has been delivered to the pathology laboratory and is cut for examination for tumor. A "touch-prep slide" is made by taking a slide and touching it against the tissue to produce an imprint. A slice of tissue, usually no thicker than three-sixteenths of an inch, is then placed in what is known as a "chuck." Solutions are then placed around it, and the chuck is put into a -20 to -23 degrees centigrade cryostat, a machine that causes rapid freezing. In about three minutes the specimen is frozen solid. Then the chuck is placed on a microtome, a machine that can cut extremely thin slices. The microtone cuts slices approximately ten microns thick. Ten microns is about one and one half times the diameter of a human red blood cell. Next, the cut section is removed from the microtome and placed on a slide where it is immersed for ten seconds in wood alcohol. The slide is then run through a standard rapid-staining procedure and a small glass top is placed over the tissue to protect it. At this time, the touch-prep slide is also stained. The purpose of the frozen-section slide is to examine the structure of the tissue rapidly, and that of the touch-prep imprint slide to examine the cellular structure. These two slides should agree.

Meg is still unconscious, unaware of the pathologist working against time. She is almost certainly unaware that her fate in terms of what will happen to her left breast is being decided in a twenty-minute procedure—a procedure with the potential for inaccuracy.

Yet Meg Land's fate is dependent at this moment on accuracy. In the frozen technique, the histological appearance and cell architecture are considerably distorted. This distortion occurs because of the freezing process, shrinking in alcohol, and the fact that the stain is a rapidly performed one. The stain is not as good as that in a permament section. The technical appearance of the tissue is not of the highest quality. The tissue is wrinkled, torn, and fractured by the cutting processes of the frozen method. All these difficulties are things the pathologist must "read through." In other words, the pathologist must make decisions based on examination of tissue that has been distorted by the way it has been processed. He must be able to understand which of the changes he sees are processing distortions, or "artifacts," and which changes are due to the actual abnormalities of the tissue.

Although the pathologist can detect cancer by means of frozen section, it is difficult, if not impossible, to classify the cancer. This is discussed in the Appendix: "The Breast Cancer Problem." Classifying, or determining the type of a cancer, can give the physician or surgeon a better idea of what the prognosis of Meg's disease might be, and therefore might alter the direction of its treatment.

Moreover, even if Meg were not lying unconscious and anesthetized, she would be one of the last people in the world permitted to review a pathologist's work. She is simply not a doctor. Had Meg been a physician, or had her surgeon been more familiar with the pathology laboratory, they might have made a crucial observation: pathologists are not infallible. Of course, the pathologist's degree of experience is directly proportional to his accuracy and diagnostic skills. But his high degree of specialization may isolate him from the overall picture—from the *total patient.*

Has Meg's surgeon reviewed recent literature? Has he for example ever come across the invaluable perspectives put forward both in a paper and in a book on cancer by Dr. Roger Terry, chief surgical pathologist at Los Angeles County Hospital? Terry suggests that pathologists should be doctors first and experts on diseased tissue second.

Pathologists can serve patients and other doctors best if their situation encourages communication and offers every opportunity for the pathologist to obtain adequate clinical data concerning all aspects of the patient's history. Dr. Terry also makes the point that not all laboratory technologists are equally skillful. It follows from this that he is convinced the pathologist should use the best available technical staff and coordinate with them to produce the best possible tissue sections for microscopic interpretation.

Dr. Terry points out that the technologists, or the people who process the tissue, are fallible too. They sometimes commit important errors in processing tissue (including, believe it or not, identifying a specimen with the wrong patient). Occasionally a technician may fail to properly imbed the part of the tissue from which the diagnosis is made, so that, unfortunately, the pathologist never sees the correct section of the tissue.

When the biopsy technique is poor, or when the tissue fails to include the diagnostic background to the tumor, even the best processing techniques cannot produce an adequate specimen for diagnosis. For example, did Meg's surgeon handle the excised tissue from Meg's breast with the utmost gentleness? Did he perhaps affect the tissue by putting undue pressure or heat on it, thus causing injury to it which may preclude adequate diagnosis? These are all things to consider.

If Meg's surgeon had been seated with the pathologist as he examined the slide, he would have been aware that examing a microscopic slide is like looking at a single frame of a movie. It may sometimes be possible to deduce from that single frame what has been happening, but finally only a guess can be made as to how the plot or disease may subsequently develop.

Obviously, too, and despite what many may think, no pathologist is always right. The surgeon can, however, expect a carefully considered "opinion," known as a diagnosis, of the abnormal tissue. It is unfortunate that Meg Land's surgeon is not present in the pathologist's laboratory so that he might discuss the diagnosis with the pathologist.

As Dr. Terry observes, it is evident that tumor diagnosis should not be a guessing game when, at the extreme, the patient's life— and, at the minimum, the *quality* of her life—is at stake. All data, clinical history, laboratory findings, and X-ray information must be shared between the pathologist and other physicians. Ideally, each surgeon should review all biopsy specimens directly with the pathologist, which would prove a joint educational process and provide for the most accurate diagnosis possible for the benefit of women like Meg Land.

A Rapid Treatment

The twenty-minute diagnosis of tissue taken from Meg's left breast at eight o'clock Friday morning was "infiltrating ductal carcinoma." Meg Land, forty-two-year-old female, wife of Barry Land, mother of four children, was minutes away from a drastic and profound change in her life. Her surgeon had decided to perform what is known as a Halsted radical mastectomy. It is not a small operation. It is deforming. It is not just a loss of the breast. There are immense emotional and physical overtones.

Figure 1

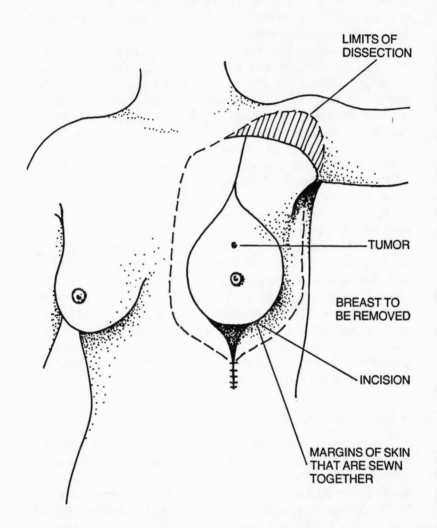

LIMITS OF
DISSECTION

TUMOR

BREAST TO
BE REMOVED

INCISION

MARGINS OF SKIN
THAT ARE SEWN
TOGETHER

LINES OF INCISION FOR A RADICAL MASTECTOMY
This illustration shows where the surgeon will make incisions to remove the breast. This is a vertical incision. If reconstruction is con-
templated, some surgeons say that a horizontal incision is better.

The air of the operating room has totally changed now. Everyone is in motion. The surgeon has rescrubbed, changed gowns and gloves. New sterile instrument trays are uncovered. Meg's outstretched left arm is fitted with a sterile stocking. Her left breast and chest area are swabbed again with soap—and the chest area is redraped with new sterile cloths.

The time is eight thirty A.M. The senior surgeon discusses the incision line with his junior assistant, and with a sterile blue marking pen outlines the area he will cut with the new scalpel. (See figure 1, page 36.) As he cuts deeper and deeper into the breast tissue, a suction tube is employed that leads to a bottle used to measure the amount of blood lost. The sponges used to soak up blood were counted beforehand, and are counted again as they are used and hung up on a chrome rack.

Barry Land looks at his watch and wonders why his wife has not returned. He thinks to himself that he hasn't been in a hospital since Meg had their fourth child, and he feels oddly out of place in this strange green and antiseptic-smelling room. He lights a cigarette—if only to be doing something. He walks to the window and tries to watch the passing cars, but his thoughts keep flashing back to Meg. He tries to focus on the proposal he'd been working on, but somehow he feels a wariness, an instinctive foreboding— the proposal suddenly doesn't seem important to him at all. He stops a nurse in the hall and asks about his wife. The nurse replies crisply, "I'm sorry, sir, we don't think she's out of the operating room yet." The nurse turns and walks down the hallway. Barry returns to the room and collapses in a green vinyl armchair. He has no idea what is happening to his wife.

This is what the Halsted radical mastectomy is about to mean to Meg Land: the breast will be completely removed. Both her pectoral muscles will be removed. As many nodes as possible under her arm will be removed. (See figures 2 and 3, pages 38 and 39.)

Figure 2

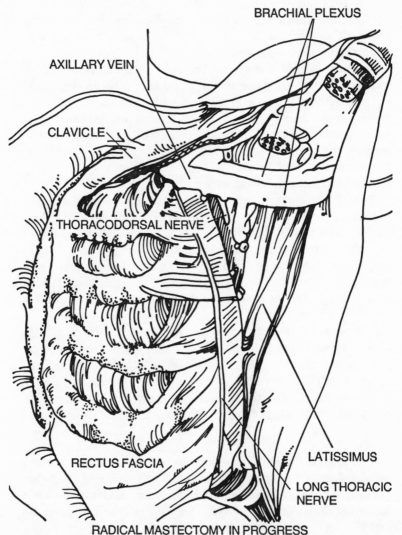

RADICAL MASTECTOMY IN PROGRESS

Here the surgeon has already removed the breast, pectoral muscles, and lymph nodes in the axilla. What is left, as you can see, is the chest wall, the deep blood vessels, the nerves of the axilla, and thin flaps of skin which will be used to cover this large defect.

Figure 3

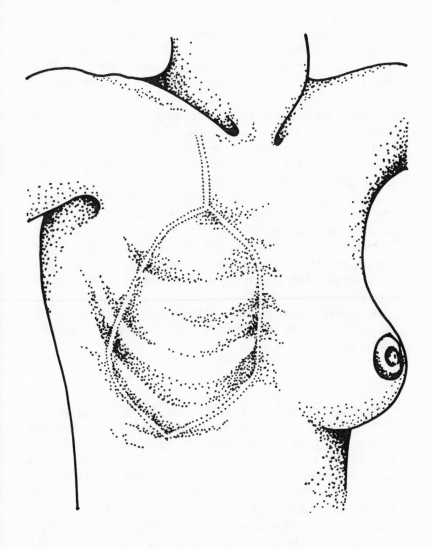

Chest wall after radical mastectomy—a good result (with skin graft).

The breast was removed. A deformed area was left. It was and is not pretty. The surgeon had removed both of Meg's left pectoral muscles; the result was a completely sunken area. She will no longer be able to wear low-cut clothes. The removal of the fatty tissues and glandular tissues from the armpit (axilla) will probably interfere with the natural drainage of lymph from Meg's left arm. Perspiration may cease. She can possibly expect swelling of the arm.

The operation was completed, and Meg was semiconscious as she was wheeled into the recovery room. Meanwhile Barry has received no word other than the fact that his wife was first "still in surgery" and then "in the recovery room for some time yet." Barry has no idea why the biopsy is taking so long.

At last the surgeon comes into the room in his green scrub suit. He introduces himself with a firm handshake, "Mr. Land, we have some bad news for you."

Barry has never even seen the surgeon before. When he visited his wife last night, the surgeon had already come and gone.

"Your wife has cancer, sir, and we had to remove her left breast. . . . I think we got it all."

Barry stands staring at this stranger who has just announced to him that his wife has cancer and that she no longer has one of her breasts.

"What in hell does *that* all mean?"

The surgeon now looks at Barry Land, his litany broken.

"Just what I said, sir."

Barry is stunned. He asks again, "But what does it mean?"

Now the surgeon looks distinctly rushed and bored—he didn't want to have to go into all the details. It has reached the psychological stage, so he dips into his storehouse of homilies and comes out with the direct approach. "It means that your wife has cancer, that I removed her left breast in order to get the cancer out. Obviously, she'll have to take awhile to recover, Mr. Land. The extent of the surgery will come as a big surprise to her. And you can be very comforting to her over the next few days. I'm sure she'll do just fine," he continues, extending Barry a hand and a philosophical smile. "If there are any questions, contact my office. Are there any now?"

"No," Barry mumbled, before he had fully understood the surgeon's question, and with that the surgeon nodded and left the room. It is a confused and utterly unprepared man who slumps in room 608's chair. He waits.

A young nurse comes into the room.

"Is there any news about my wife? When will she be coming back from the recovery room?"

The nurse stops, says she doesn't know, departing with words that confuse Barry Land even more: "I'm sorry, sir, about your wife." As the nurse is halfway out the door of the room, she stops and says, "Sometimes, Mr. Land, it helps if you tell them you still love them."

"I'm not entirely clear what you mean, miss. Why do you say that?" he asks wearily.

The nurse frames her answer thoughtfully. "Well, sir, losing a breast is a major event for a woman."

Barry smiles weakly after her departing figure.

Meg's first hours after the operation are filled with fuzzy pain. Lying there, questions of all sorts and sizes filtered into her consciousness, but she is able to push them behind pain and drugs. Now, for just a moment, she hears "him" speak—it is the surgeon. "No complications . . . you're doing fine. . . . I'm sure we got it all."

Later, in the foggy limbo of recovery, she slowly awakens. Seeing the cumbersome bandages, she builds false hopes in herself that the breast is still as it always was . . . a part of her. Her self-deception soon passes, though, and she knows her breast is gone. Amputated. She looks down her bed and sees a strange, round, plastic holder of reddish fluid with plastic tubing leading up underneath her cumbersome bandages. The tubing is a drain installed to ensure the proper evacuation of fluids from the area that was once Meg's breast. She is shocked. A nurse sedates her into another world. It provides a brief respite.

The worst has happened. Meg Land is totally unprepared. When she reaches a fully conscious level, after the operation, depression sets in. As the dressings are changed for the first time, she is aware of the powerful odor—the odor of surgery. Visually, the breast that was "nothing to worry about" has been replaced by something she is totally unprepared to see. She no longer has an ability to disassociate herself from what has happened to her body. The former breast area is now a gashed and swollen plain, broken by a track of ugly black sutures extending across her chest. She looks away. She will not look again. It is not pretty.

"Why, why me?" she gasps. But there is no one to talk to, no one to rescue her from the prison of her mind. The physical recovery is beginning, but the mental anguish intensifies as alone she confronts two of the worst calamities of her life. She has cancer, and only one breast.

Her surgeon visits, rambling on incessantly, "Nice healing. . . . You'll be happy to know that none of your nodes were positive. . . . You're really very lucky." Meg's eyes are red and swollen, and she can cry no more. She stares at the flowers on her bedside table. She wants him to leave her alone—to stop talking about "how lucky she is," "how wonderful things are." She is desperate, angry, alone. It all went too fast. It is not hard for Meg to dismiss everyone who comes near her—they simply don't exist—even her husband. The gap between them was widened.

Meg's surgeon never gives her emotional state a thought. "She'll snap out of it—they always do," he tells Barry. But Meg has lost more than a breast. She has lost a symbol of her womanhood, her sex, her motherhood, her wifehood. The bra stuffed on the empty left side with cotton and gauze is a poor substitute in her eyes. She still will not look at the scar.

She hates the nurses who come to her and smilingly encourage her to use her painful arm. How could they possibly know. Anger is barely suppressed. How could they say everything was all right? She hates the words "I see we are doing better today." *Nothing* is all right. She feels that the already tenuous hold she and her husband have on their relationship will be inevitably weakened.

As long as Meg is bandaged and removed from the world, in the recovery process, she keeps her questions to a minimum, but soon they will outweigh the pain. The conversations with the surgeons and the nurses always end up the same: "You're getting along fine," "Of course, you'll be getting back to normal in a few weeks."

By now Meg Land does not believe anyone. She is left alone to deal with frightfully serious and real questions. How will her husband react to her mutilated body? Will sex be the same? Could anyone, even her husband, bear to look at her body again? What will she tell the children? Will people notice? Why is the area draining so much? Is that normal? Will the swelling ever go down? Self-pity creeps in, making the questions more demeaning. Strangely enough, as the recovery progresses, Meg is even more intensely aware of her disability. The natural balance she once had with both breasts is now gone. She lists to one side. The skin of her arm is stretched with swelling. Meg cannot move her arm without feeling pain. She is told she can possibly expect swelling of her arm, and that she needs to be constantly on the alert for any small cuts, bites, or anything that could lead to infections, since the arm will now be prone to trouble owing to the lack of proper circulation. Even something as minor as the onset of hot weather could cause the arm to swell with fluids. She must learn to walk properly and be fitted with an artificial breast. An artificial breast! Meg is expected to cope with this permanent scar—this loss—as casually as if she had lost an appendix. Chin up. Carry on. Get the house back to normal. Face an incomplete body with a smile. Cope with the misunderstanding and feelings of private terror. And soon the day will come when she will be forced to leave the sanctuary of the hospital's insulated world, and go home. Meg has no idea where to start—what to do.

There is no one at this time to share the pain. All the emotions, anger, fears, frustration, and tears are locked into a mind the medical profession has refused to acknowledge. Had her husband returned wounded from war, his care would have been more honorable and sensitive.

Barry is totally bewildered. He has no idea what to say to his wife. He daily performs rituals of bringing flowers and books to Meg in the hospital. There is no conversation between them about what has taken place. Neither of them can even begin to talk about it. Neither of them has been the least bit prepared.

Meg Land, educated, healthy, assured of the extent of her knowledge of breast cancer, is beginning to discover she knows nothing of the disease or its implications. For example, she has never heard or read about a report by a patient education committee that identified problems found in a group study of mastectomy patients at a major hospital. The group participants revealed a great body of problems they had faced after their operations. The following concerns were mentioned most frequently in the sessions:

Pain, soreness, aches from both recent and past surgery and radiation; problems with their arms, which included swelling, aching, tiredness, heaviness, inability to lift things, and the lack of full range of motion; general body weakness and tiredness; nervousness; trouble sleeping because of the absence of a breast; inability to get comfortable in bed; nausea and constipation; back pain; menopausal problems; questions about how to exercise and when to start; questions about activities and exercises; continuity of care and apprehension about seeing new doctors, feeling that they were left out on their own after discharge from the hospital; and a desire for more sensitive staff, including doctors, nurses, and clerks.

Since Meg knew neither of the study, nor of the conclusions of the group, she would feel a particular loss when alone, or when several of these problems confronted her. Particularly and unnecessarily, she would feel increasingly alone. Meg and Barry Land knew, because they were told, that her operation was a Halsted radical mastectomy. She did not know, because she did not trouble to investigate and learn beforehand, and because alternative methods of surgery were not explained to her, that there were other options. Meg was not aware that more surgeons were leaning toward a *modified radical mastectomy,* which is essentially the same operation as the *classic (or Halsted) radical mastectomy.* In the *modified,* the nodes in the armpit are removed; however, the pectoral muscles are left intact. This type of operation would have offered functional advantages for Meg when weighed against the more radical procedure; the arm usually remains strong and there is usually little postoperative swelling or edema of the arm. It is the leaving of the pectoral muscles that is so important cosmetically, because it preserves untouched the natural fold in front of the armpit. Also, Meg would have had a chance with this operation for planned breast reconstruction. The sparing of the pectoral muscles additionally makes the possibility of breast reconstruction more favorable, for it provides additional padding over an implant, should one be inserted during breast reconstruction at a later date.

Meg did not know about the *extended simple mastectomy.* The breast is removed, as well as some of the lymph nodes in the axilla. This is called "sampling," or "cherry picking," the nodes in order to check for cancer. This technique is often followed by administration of some form of chemotherapy or radiation therapy.

Meg knew nothing about the *simple mastectomy,* which does not disturb the pectoral muscles or the lymph nodes. This procedure does not usually cause swelling of the arm and limitation of motion of the shoulder. The simple mastectomy does not, however, check the axillary nodes for possible cancer.

Meg was not told about the *partial mastectomy,* in which the lump and the section of surrounding breast tissue are removed. After this kind of surgery, the breast shape is fairly normal, but the visual outcome depends on the size of the lump, its location and, obviously, on the general size of a woman's breast. In the case of two women with equal-sized lumps, the surgery performed on a small breast will appear to take a larger segment, whereas if it is performed on a large breast, the alteration will quite probably be less noticeable. Pain and discomfort are usually slight, and most patients can often return to the routine of their lives at home or work within a few days of the operation. With this type of surgery, however, some breast tissue containing cancer may be left behind. Some cancers are not confined to the lump being excised. Frequently, at the time of surgery, scattered nondetectable cancers exist throughout the breast. Once again, in the partial mastectomy, there is no investigation surgically into the axillary nodes for either removal or sampling of the cancer.

These lesser surgical procedures are frequently followed by some form of radiation therapy and/or chemotherapy.

Had Meg or Meg's doctor been particularly diligent in exploring options, she would also have known about the *subcutaneous mastectomy*. Surgeons seldom use this mode of surgery. It is meant to be employed only in properly selected cases. It entails removing the inside breast tissue only, leaving the skin, nipple, and pectoral muscles intact. This permits a breast implant to be inserted beneath the skin at the time of surgery or at a later date, attempting to reproduce the natural breast contour.

This operation is most often practiced for women with "noninvasive carcinoma, Type I." Such noninvasive cancer usually has no tendency to *metastasize* (spread) into other parts of the breast, axillary nodes, and so forth. This surgical method is also used for severe, persistent fibrocystic disease and related problems. It may be less traumatic for the woman who is subjected to multiple biopsies for benign disease.

Some forward-looking physicians and surgeons have theorized that in the future, subcutaneous mastectomy will be feasible in combination with immunotherapy and/or chemotherapy to control breast cancer.

Finally, Meg might have been told of the *lumpectomy*. The operation consists merely of the removal of the breast lump itself and some surrounding tissue. Usually this procedure is followed by some form of radiation therapy of the remaining breast tissue and axillary nodes, leaving a more normal-looking breast. Lumpectomy remains the subject of controversy.

Meg Land did not understand the basic nature of her cancer— nor do the doctors. The exact cause is not known. We do not know, nor can we predict, the type of spread. No laboratory method exists to discover distant tumor while it is still microscopic. Thus, any clinical type of classification is somewhat unpredictable. We cannot explain spontaneous regression of a cancer. We cannot explain sudden, explosive metastatic spread of breast cancer. In sum, and in honesty, we have to admit that we know little about breast cancer other than that it often kills the patient. *However, properly guided treatment can modify the course of the cancer and possibly the length of survival of the patient.*

Sadly, even if Meg had known her options, the conscientious physician would have to tell her of the difficulty of recommending one technique over another. What she should have been left with is this: *She should have been aware of her options and possible decisions concerning the type of treatment.* If her surgeon could not comply with this method of informing his patients, then he should have assisted Meg in selecting a surgeon who could best respond to her needs. Obviously, she should have been aware of all the pros and cons of each surgical procedure.

Meg was also unaware of the many possible forms of combined surgery and radiation, or surgery and chemotherapy, or surgery and immunotherapy—or a combination of all the above. She began her breast cancer ordeal unaware, and was informed after the fact. Now Meg would bravely withhold criticism, but she had not been allowed to be an active and informed participant in the vital decisions affecting her body. She had been rushed into surgery as though hers were an emergency situation. It was not. It was important that something be done quickly, but there was no need for incredible haste. She had not time to discuss the situation with her husband, had that been possible within the limited parameters of their communication.

Meg Land had not been active participant in her own destiny.

Perhaps one of the worst aspects of Meg's rushed surgery was that she was not checked for widespread cancer *before* her radical surgery. Should Meg later show up with widespread cancer, some months after surgery, she would have had needlessly aggressive surgery. In other words, there would have been no hope at the time of surgery of curing the cancer by removing the breast—the cancer would already have traveled beyond the limits of the breast and into the body. Had Meg's surgeon performed a metastatic workup before surgery, and had this workup proved positive, he would have chosen a lesser operation. Meg was also uninformed about the *necessity* of those *vital tests to check for cancer present elsewhere in her body*. And these tests, even if negative, would have provided a "baseline study" to compare with future tests.

Meg is now a cancer victim. Se will remain so far the rest of her life. She will have to be followed with the utmost attention by her surgeon and doctor. Because the operation is over, she is now in the highest-risk category possible for either recurrent breast cancer or widespread cancer. Her life has changed because of cancer and the loss of a breast. But her battle has just begun. The follow-up care must be an integral part of her life, sometimes more than twice a year. This is something else Meg was never told. She has not been "cured" by her optimistic and insensitive surgeon—she must learn to live with the examination, the fears, the cancer, and the possibility of death. She will live from one clean bill of health to the next, for years and years. Meg will have to become ultrasensitive to her own body—to any aches, pains, or weight loss. She and her surgeon and her family doctor will of necessity be forever suspicious of the errant cells and their possible reemergence. The story of Meg Land and her disease will last her lifetime. It is unforgivable that something so major was made to be something so minor by those who came into medical contact with her.

Picking up the Pieces

Meg Land knew she had had her breast removed. She was not aware of the alternatives she had available besides a classical radical mastectomy. *She did not understand the importance of communication—that it could be the best ally she could possibly have had.* As a cancer patient—and Meg is now a cancer patient —she carries as an immense burden, of the thought of possible death. She needs now, certainly more than at any other time in her life, to express her feelings and those things important to her. Too many women set aside their real feelings and assume a stoic pose —trying to convince themselves and others that they are in control. These women seem to feel it is somehow wrong to say, "I need help." The woman who is likely to suffer most is one who will not voice her depression. She loops back and forth emotionally, hiding her true feelings, pretending she is on top of the situation in front of her physician, her family, and everyone else around her.

The fact of having cancer is unchangeable. Regardless of the choice of form of treatment, the period during and immediately after any sort of cancer treatment is unequivocally the most important for a woman—days that set the tone for the rest of her life.

Some have suggested how a woman like Meg Land should regain her equilibrium: Accept the loss of a breast by fully mourning that loss; regenerate a self-image worthy of love and the rewards of life; begin to make peace with the possible recurrence of cancer. However, that is a tall order! It is admirable if anyone can manage even one step of that process. A woman who has breast cancer must necessarily test strengths never before encountered. The stark reality of losing a breast is a major trauma to the mind and emotions. Meg could well be in a constant state of depression, anger, disassociation, irrational behavior, and possibly a preoccupation with the thought of death. She may isolate herself from her family and friends—trapped within the prison of her mind. It is understandable, and she should not be put under further stress by being punished by anyone for having those feelings.

At this moment in Meg's life she should not consider it a sign of weakness to ask for help—psychiatric help, help from a social worker, or help from another woman who has encountered the same problems. If Meg saw a person drowning, she would surely try to help. In exactly the same way, if Meg is drowning in despair and anxiety, there is obviously nothing wrong in asking someone to help save her.

Meg must now understand that the surgeon and hospital staff should approach her with as much psychological assistance as possible. As much as a woman may need and want help, she may not be able to ask for it. Whenever this is the case, the imperative is clear: Everyone who knows someone who has breast cancer must spend a little extra time with her. Even those cancer victims who will not discuss the situation with anyone will at least benefit from some warmth and support.

Many hospitals are set up in large cities to approach the woman in a team way. But Meg is being "controlled" by her surgeon. No staff, social worker, or psychologist can approach a patient without the surgeon's approval. Some surgeons are aware of the team programs, but either do not give orders for the team (and this includes Reach to Recovery) to swing into action, or simply feel such teams should be ignored. It is impossible to understand such a surgeon's rationale, when his concern should be the recovery of the total patient. Often, the woman or her family will have to ask for help, but many never even know that help exists.

Here is a case history that could exactly represent Meg Land. It describes some of the thoughts and feelings of a patient who didn't or couldn't ask for help until long after radical surgery:

The only data that my brain registered were that suddenly one day I was perfectly fine—I was happy, smiling, playing with the children. Then, out of the blue, it seemed as if my life had ended. To those who looked at me I seemed to be perfectly all right physically. But I was going through horrendous mental torture. Yes, physically on the outside, I was fine. I looked great. But inside, I was caught within the prison of my mind—knowing that I no longer had a breast. My husband and I had never communicated much on a level that was warm or open. His idea of my being sick, my not being able to accomplish certain things around the house as I had before the operation . . . seemed strange and foreign to him. While I was in the hospital, things seemed to go very smoothly—he provided me with love and attention and flowers—but when I got home, it was a different story. I was angry, I was depressed, and I took it out on everyone around me. I was also extremely fatigued day after day after day. I couldn't seem to get my old vigor back again. The relations between my husband and myself took a turn for the worse. I felt that he rejected me because I no longer had a breast. We could not talk about it. The children were the worst off, I suppose. Those little ones knew of my absence from the house, they knew I had been in the hospital, and what returned home was certainly not the same mother. I snapped at them. I was angry with them a great deal of the time. My husband and I decided not to tell the children that I had ever had cancer. As I look back now, I can see it was certainly a mistake. The children weren't dumb, and they listened in to phone calls and discussions with neighbors about my surgery. They felt left out, confused—and rightly so. It took me over three years after my surgery to finally learn to deal with the fact that the threat of death hung over me day and night. Somehow, I came to live with that threat better than I lived with the fact that I had one breast. I felt that life became so difficult, I really went into a serious depression—I stopped cleaning the house, buying clothes —I arranged each day as though there really was no tomorrow.

I pushed everyone and everything aside. As I look back now, I see that if I had been able to speak with a psychologist at the time of the surgery, and if there had been an interval between the biopsy and the surgery. I think I would have been able to deal with my family, particularly my husband, in a more realistic manner. As it stands now, I am very sad to have lost so many years of living while establishing myself in a cocoon of depression and anger. There are so many years that I lost— not being completely with my husband, my children, and myself.

These words were spoken by a woman in the medical profession—a woman who is medically sophisticated, and certainly actively involved with her patients' accepting medical misfortunes. The emotional impact of a mastectomy for women who know less about medical aspects must therefore be all the greater. One respected study reports that more than half of their sampling of women who have had mastectomy have admitted severe anxiety or depression. C. J. Ervin, who wrote *The Psychological Adjustment to Mastectomy,* advanced the theory that emotional suffering far outweights the actual physical suffering in mastectomy patients.

Our society in particular attaches tremendous importance to the female breast, so its loss causes many women to feel they are no longer really feminine. Furthermore, these feelings of femininity loss are constantly thrown in a woman's face by the advertising media, not to mention during normal conversations or sexual intercourse. There are no real figures available concerning what really goes on between a mastectomy patient and her husband in terms of their sexual life. Studies have found women especially reluctant to discuss this intimate area. If a woman is single, the fears associated with breast loss, and concern over her sexual desirability and possible future sexual relations are magnified. Here is a case with which Meg Land would empathize—a single woman, thirty-four years old, who had a radical mastectomy. She expressed her dilemma eloquently.

It was a devastating experience to have lost my breast, and I thought there was no other option. For well over a year I didn't date any men, and closed off my past relationships with other male friends. Any time I encountered a man who gave me a smile—perhaps asked me to lunch—my reaction was normal. But a split second later, I would be overcome by the fact that I did not have a breast, and I certainly did not know how to tell a man that I did not have a breast. I continued for two more years not seeing men. I have been in psychotherapy now for eight months and have talked to many other women who are single and have had mastectomies. I still feel awkward about the fact that I have no breast, and certainly in relation to men. However, I feel that I am perhaps beginning to deal better with this. I wish that I had been able to speak with someone before I had my surgery, and I wish I had known there was an option for something less than a radical. . . . I would have played the odds.

According to a well-known researcher in the field of psychology of breast cancer, women have a strong feeling about the remaining breast. The breast may be cherished as a symbol of nuturing motherhood, or a sign of femininity—and it is pointed out that the breast is an important psychosexual symbol. In many women, the remaining breast serves as a nonfunctioning organ. Some women will not allow it to be caressed during the sexual act, preferring to keep on their brassiere, never undressing. Moreover, many experience a gravity problem with body symmetry. A woman with a fairly large or pendulous breast remaining after a mastectomy must relearn to walk and alter her modality of balance. This also falls into the realm of rehabilitation, which will be discussed later.
And what of Meg Land's husband and his equal need to com-

municate his concerns about the survival of his wife? How should he respond to her at home after surgery? What kinds of needs will Meg have and, in general, what can he do to help her adjust? Not a great deal in the literature has been presented on this problem, except in extremely general terms.

What we know at this time—data particularly gained from interviews with both women and professional staff—suggests that the attending surgeons and staff should attempt to include the husband (or the predominant male member in the relationship) as closely as possible in the breast cancer experience, since he, too, is often in an emotional crisis stage. The male is often totally left out of the decision-making policies concerning his wife, and has little or no understanding of what is taking place or how serious a matter it can be. Neither Meg Land nor her husband had ever considered this, nor could they have been expected to, since no physician they came in contact with offered the problem for discussion.

The man may also be confused, and clearly may respond in kind to the unusual behavior of his wife. If she acts hostile to him because of her loss, he may well be just as hostile to her in response because he has no insight into what is really going on in her mind and heart. Every effort should be made to attune Meg's husband to the role he can expect to play. For example, it would have been a great help for Barry to be able to speak openly, not only with the attending physician, but also with a psychologist, as to the sort of emotional problems he might encounter at home. In his own anxiety, he may retreat from the questions that beset him: What kind of prognosis his wife may have, how he should react, how he should handle the emotional upsets at home, not only those of his wife, but the inevitable problems with the children. His responsibility is also a heavy burden. He must also live with the constant fear that his wife has cancer, and with the possibility of her ultimate loss. He must struggle along with her as new treatments are begun, possible physical and psychological setbacks occur, or the prolonged severe illness that often accompanies the patient's last months sets in.

Many husbands have stated that they never felt closer to their wives than during the cancer experience, yet at the same time never so far away.

Some institutions and clinics have attempted to set up group discussions for husbands and lovers—males only. Their participants have said that these groups have indeed lessened the anxiety accompanying the situation, and that it is generally helpful to know that other men have the same trials to experience.

So Meg's husband, who should not have been forgotten, has found himself forgotten. He has his needs and fears as intense as her own. If he could talk and learn about what is happening, or what could happen, it would mean that a unified support system has been carried into the private confines of the husband-wife relationship in the home. A single battle of emotions, fears, frustrations, angers, depressions, and love could be shared. Barry Land could have been, and should have been, prepared and aware. He did not have to remain alone.

Suppose, though, that Meg's husband, and indeed the rest of her family, continue to refuse to involve themselves in the discussion of the darker side of life, especially weakness or sickness. If a woman's family is structured this way, her loneliness, sense of abandonment, and isolation are multiplied a dozen times over—driving her to the point of suicide. Then the woman, angry or depressed, yet feeling a need to be dependent, has no possible avenue for resolution of her feelings. She cannot ask her husband or family to hear or understand her anger, much less allow her to become a dependent person, though she is at a weak point and needs an abundance of love and acceptance. A physician cannot know how a family is structured. A family, marriage, or household is often complex. But the basic point is simple: Once Meg had learned she must have a biopsy, she should at least have attempted to discuss her fears, emotions, and feelings about the situation with her husband and, if possible, with the family. When a woman finds herself in a position in which this is impossible, or in which her husband doesn't seem to care or to realize the emotional significance of the situation, she should by all means seek outside help. Of paramount importance is talking with someone—even a crisis telephone line, a neighbor, or a minister. *Talk to someone! Living in private terror is not necessary today.*

The family can be of utmost importance to the woman who has discovered a breast lump. If they are informed of all aspects of what a breast biopsy entails, then avenues for discussion and understanding are more open should the woman prove to have breast cancer. Meg's surgeon should not have felt threatened by her desire for her own and her family's involvement in a decision that affects her life. If anything, that involvement makes for a patient who is more trusting and confident in her surgeon's judgment. The knowledge that a physician cares about the *total woman*—her feelings about her body, and her destiny—will instill and enhance her confidence in the surgeon. This involvement should also continue if a woman needs other medical treatment such as radiation or chemotherapy.

Some women, however, will frankly say that they do not wish involvement in any decision-making policies. It is also possible that in some cases because of preexisting serious physiological or psychological problems a woman should be sheltered from unnecessary details of her physical condition. The patient, however, will generally be a guide as to how much about the disease she does want to know.

It is widely recognized in the medical community that half of cancer patients "know" what their condition is if they are in serious or possible terminal states. Furthermore, one study indicated that almost 90 percent of the patients with cancer wanted to be told the truth.

So even if Meg had failed in her own responsibilities concerning self-knowledge, *she should have been informed of her options regarding treatment. She should also have been informed of any side effects of any treatment she might receive.* The reason is simple:

Usually the better prepared the patient, the better she will endure the psychological as well as the physical trials of her illness. It is a moral law, if not a statute, that physicians are obligated to inform their patients about their options and possible side effects of their disease unless otherwise indicated.

For Meg Land, as for most women, the time spent in discussion and adjustment to possible surgery is usually limited by how busy their surgeon is, revealing a serious lack of continuity in medical care. The woman is shocked by the impending encounter with major surgery that the biopsy results represent; she doesn't really understand what's going on. She is rushed. *Adequate and personally tailored time must be spent by the physician with the woman before scheduling her for the biopsy. And after the biopsy, discussion must follow of what will be necessary treatment if a malignant lump is discovered.*

And when a malignancy is discovered, women need extra time to discuss the possibility of cancer treatment with their families, other physicians, psychologists, social workers, or clergymen. Meg was not given this time, and the importance of drawing in her husband and children or whoever may have been emotionally close to her cannot be overestimated. It is a necessity. The discovery of cancer is a crisis, and a woman needs as much assistance as she can possibly gather. The problems must be dealt with one at a time, so that the woman can be as comfortable as possible in solving them. This one-step-at-a-time approach is certainly much better than having later to pick up and reassemble emotional shards after a woman has been railroaded into a decision she was unsure about by the traditional surgeon who says, "Let's get it over with—we'll have to operate immediately or it will spread and you will surely die."

A healthy resolution for Meg would be possible only if she were actively involved in solving her problems—not if she avoids them. It is impossible for a woman to reach a solution that will have a happy outcome if she insists there has been no problem or, even worse, if a physician has led her to believe that "it's no problem."

Possible breast cancer *is a problem,* and if a physician lacks the time or motivation to assist his patient in this crisis, he ought to refer her to a physician who has that time and important concern.

Not to be overlooked is the reason behind a delay between the biopsy and, if needed, cancer treatment. For breast cancer, this means that the process of treating the disease is divided into two parts. First, a biopsy is performed, prefarably under local anesthesia (unless otherwise indicated). Then there is a delay of a few days in which the biopsy specimen is carefully studied. If the diagnosis is cancer, the second stage is a workup to check the body for cancer that might have spread. Then definitive treatment can be planned. The type of treatment that is instituted depends on the decisions of the doctors and the patient, made in light of the overall situation.

Breaking the treatment of breast cancer into two parts this way, especially if a local anesthesia is used, offers compelling advantages: Three out of four women with breast lumps will not be subjected to the additional dangers and expense of a general anesthesia, since their lumps will prove benign. Every woman who undergoes a breast biopsy will not have to face the possibility that she will wake up without a breast. Why should she undergo this terror if it's not necessary? It allows time for proper, careful study of the tumor specimen, to ensure the diagnosis is correct.

If the diagnosis is cancer, there is time for the scans, tests, and examinations that are necessary to determine if there is detectable cancer in other parts of the body. If it can be proven that cancer has already spread to other organs such as the liver or bones, attempts to cure it by radical surgery will fail. Thus, there is no need to subject a patient to radical surgery. In other words, if you can't cure the patient, why go out of your way to mutilate her? There is time for the doctor to carefully plan his treatment rather than rushing into one or another course of action. The cancer patient has the opportunity, if she wishes, to participate to some extent in the choice of treatment for her. She has a chance to obtain more information on which to base a valid decision. There is time to prepare her psychologically for her treatment. This method saves a lot of the doctor's time. This is because in the "One-Step Procedure" (see One-Stage Procedure, page 197) the doctor has to inform the patient about what the mastectomy means prior to doing a biopsy, since if the frozen-section exam is positive for cancer, he will be doing a mastectomy immediately. In the medical-legal climate that now exists in the Untied States, a doctor is obliged to inform his patients about all the possible side effects that could reasonably result from the treatment he is going to institute. For a mastectomy, this discussion is long and gory. Why should the doctor have to waste his time telling this to the three out of four women who won't have cancer? Why should they have to hear it? His time is perhaps better spent with the one out of four who *will* have cancer. Moreover, money is saved by the patients with benign lumps. If the patient is to have a biopsy only, such things as typing and cross-matching blood for transfusions are unnecessary. Also, the expense of using an operating room equipped for major surgery is avoided, since the biopsy using local anesthetic can be performed in less elaborately equipped surgical rooms.

At present, this scheme of treatment for breast cancer is used mainly at hospitals that are affiliated with medical centers, such as the Los Angeles County-University of Southern California Medical Center. The reason the two-step biopsy procedure is not not yet in widespread use is that there still exists in the general medical community a widespread belief that failure to operate immediately when breast cancer is diagnosed will greatly lessen the patient's chance of cure. *However, this belief is not supported by current medical literature,* although some surgeons cling to the idea that when the breast is opened in surgery for a biopsy, it must be removed at once if cancer is found. Their theory is that cancer cells can be "seeded" by the knife to other parts of the breast at the time of biopsy, or that the cancerous lump, while being excised through the normal breast tissue, will seed itself. There is, however, no solid proof of this theory, and it appears that survival rates have not changed when the biopsy and surgery have been separated. There are even some doctors who feel it may actually be more beneficial to leave the biopsy-cancer site alone for a few weeks before any treatment is begun—to settle things down, in a sense.

However, the author's bias is clear here. The two-stage procedure is advantageous for the many reasons already mentioned. Let the "public beware," though—stay informed.

If Meg Had Only Known

If Meg Land did not know the basics of detection of her disease, and if she did not know her options in dealing with it, she was equally ignorant of the possibility of rehabilitation. A breast cancer patient must be aware of the support system available to her after surgery. This message was not delivered sufficiently strongly to Meg. Part of the system is called "the Reach to Recovery Program," and it is designed to assist a woman's needs from the moments after surgery to follow-up at home. Reach to Recovery began many years ago, growing out of the determined efforts of one woman, Mrs. Terese Lasser. As a mastectomy patient herself, having undergone the emotional and physical experience, she saw the desperate need for more compassionate and sensitive follow-up treatment. Reach to Recovery has now been established in most cities in the United States. Its main purpose is a patient-to-patient contact between those who have had breast cancer, and are now leading active lives, and the woman who has just completed surgery. Unless the hospital uses it automatically, Reach to Recovery is not available to an individual patient unless it is requested by the attending physician during her hospital stay. These visits by former mastectomy patients are usually performed by women who are currently looking well and active. They give the recent mastectomee a psychological lift. Some researchers have suggested that this technique is vital to rehabilitation because the visitor has suffered both the physical and emotional impact of a mastectomy, and she is really the only person who can empathize, who can talk to a patient with actual knowledge and gentle understanding. The visitor can bring hope for the future. The patient can envision becoming part again of the outside world—with her family, as a totally functioning individual. There are manuals on mastectomies written for the patient by Terese Lasser and many booklets suggesting clothing—including possible types of swimwear and sports clothes.

The Reach to Recovery Program is sponsored by the American Cancer Society, and information, if not available from physician or hospital, can be supplied by the society. It has offices, facilities, and professional people to train all their visiting volunteers. A patient should be aware that there is someone available, another woman who has entered into the breast cancer experience. But Meg Land's physician did not mention this to her at the time of surgery, so she could not benefit from the program.

In addition to having had the experience, the Reach to Recovery volunteer brings with her a kit containing a temporary breast form and exercise manuals and materials. It is hoped she will be supplementing the hospital's own physical therapy team, who will help the woman to recoup her physical losses and regain her former strength.

Obviously no two women can possibly react to the emotional impact of breast surgery in the same way. The surgeon should be aware of the vast resources open to his patients. By reading available materials, the woman should get some guidelines on what is offered to her if, in fact, her physician does not mention or supply this information. And this was another of Meg Land's deprivations: She simply did not know and was not told that *the woman has a right to ask for as much help as she needs.* It is important for the woman who is returning home after surgery to know she still has that support system available. A support system, or course, involves the surgeon and quite possibly a psychologist or volunteer personnel. *The patient's release from the hospital is certainly not the end of the story. Close follow-up over ensuing years is crucial,*

regarding not only physical examinations but the well-being of the
patient's general psychological state as well.

The woman's relationship with her surgeon may well be limited
to bi-yearly physical examinations, but her emotional burden lives
with her every day. It is therefore vital that women know that
support is always available to them and their families at any time
in the follow-up period.

It was tragic enough that Meg Land was forced by her own
ignorance and the ignorance or inattention of her physician to endure quietly and alone one of women's most painful burdens. She
might at least have had some hope—might have been able to face
the world less badly bowed—had she known there is such a thing
as breast reconstruction. Unhappily, she did not know that either.

Breast reconstruction should be planned preoperatively. If the
tissue removed in a biopsy has proved malignant, if the patient
has been checked for distant disease elsewhere in the body, and
the form of treatment has been agreed upon by the physician, the
patient, and those close to her, it is then important for the surgeon
to disclose the possibility of breast reconstruction; Meg's surgeon
did not. Some women may have this breast reconstruction in mind,
but most do not know it is possible; some women, of course, consider restoration of their breast a matter of primary importance.
Various procedures have been devised for making a new breast.
Some have included either the use of or the mobilization of a portion of the intact breast. Recently, too, some specialists have en-
thusiastically placed various-sized silicone bags under the skin of
the chest wall. A further advance in this method has been the use
of inflatable plastic bags into which a sterile saline solution is injected until the prosthesis is comparable in size to the intact breast.

Of course, the reconstructed breast will not look as good as the
breast prior to mastectomy. It is unfortunate that some articles in
the popular press have indicated that a perfect-looking breast can
be expected. At present, this remains unlikely. If the patient has

more modest expectations, though, such as simple restoration of the original contour of her breast, a more normal body symmetry, she is less likely to be disappointed with reconstruction.

The importance of planning reconstruction of the breast before surgery is critical, for if the incisions are placed incorrectly by the general surgeon, the task of reconstructing the breast later will be difficult or impossible for the plastic surgeon. Not many surgeons, however, practice on-the-spot breast reconstruction. Most express an inclination to wait from six months to over a year before attempting reconstruction. They theorize that surgical manipulation at an earlier date might liberate entrapped tumor cells within the chest wall. However, there are some surgeons who feel reconstruction should be carried out as soon as possible. At this point the whole topic of breast reconstruction—pro and con—is embedded in medical controversy.

Reconstructive breast surgery, coupled with proper planning, is the only physically possible solution to the common postsurgical disfigurement problem. Some surgeons have expressed the importance of offering an opportunity for breast reconstruction to the woman. Even though the breast is removed, reconstruction can be deeply comforting. Usually it is advisable for the surgeon, unless he is extremely familiar with the incision and implant procedures, to seek the advice of a plastic surgeon.

It is of equal importance that women who have already had mastectomies be aware of the possibilities of breast reconstruction and seek the advice both of their general surgeon and of a plastic surgeon regarding its feasibility. But they had better know, too, that often the task is impossible, when there remains too little skin to work with or when the incision line was incorrectly placed by the surgeon. If one plastic surgeon feels that reconstruction is impossible, however, a woman who has had a mastectomy should not be entirely discouraged; it is possible to obtain several opinions on this matter. Common sense suggests that a plastic surgeon who deals with a large number of breast patients annually is the best choice. As you can imagine, reconstructing a breast after radical surgery is a great challenge to any surgeon, but it is best left in the hands of a plastic surgeon who is familiar with the techniques.

So we have gone through the ordeal of Meg Land—educated, aware, sick, perhaps victimized by an unplanned, unconceded series of errors made ignorantly. If only, before she discovered that lump, she could have come upon these words of Ralph E. Johnson, MD, of the National Cancer Institute, Bethesda, Maryland, she might not have been rushed so headlong into treatment. However, the odds of Meg Land's reading this article were one in a million. It appeared as an editorial in the November 29, 1974, issue of the *New England Journal of Medicine,* one of this country's most respected medical journals. The sad thing about this editorial is that it reached very few—both physicians and women. It is a powerful statement that deserves reproduction in its entirety.

Recent news regarding the wife of the President has again focused national attention on diseases collectively referred to as cancers that afflict one of every four Americans during their lifetime. Cancer of the breast alone is diagnosed in about ninety thousand new patients every year and there has been a long-standing medical debate over the relative merits of the various therapeutic methods. Often lost in the swirl of controversy over treatment has been a greatly needed emphasis on a more deliberate approach to the total patient from the onset. Whereas many examples should be cited within the field of oncology, cancer of the breast serves as an eloquent illustration.

Consider the standard sequence of events when a woman is found to have a breast mass whether on self-examination or by her physician. A biopsy is scheduled with the greatest of dispatch, and if the frozen-section, histiologic examination confirms the diagnosis of carcinoma, some form of mastectomy is immediately performed. For the present the majority of surgeons have an understandable preference for the traditional radical mastectomy since unequivocal documentation is lacking as yet that longterm survival is comparable with less aggressive surgical methods.

What requires recognition and demands stress is that a number of patients have widespread dissemination of disease that is clinically detectable at the time of initial diagnosis. When this fact is taken into consideration, it seems self-evident that the sequence of events described above warrants modification as follows: When a breast mass, suggestive of possible neoplasia, is detected, mammography should be performed in recognition of the fact that if the radiographic appearance is characteristic of a tumor, an eighty to ninety percent positive correlation will exist with the result of a biopsy; patients with clinical findings or mammographic examination highly suggestive or typical of cancer should be evaluated before biopsy with non-invasive diagnostic studies such as radiological skeletal survey and bone scan; if obvious metastatic disease is apparent before biopsy, operations can be limited to an excisional diagnostic biopsy or even needle biopsy under local anesthesia in some hospitals where the latter is practiced. Under some conditions, simple and local removal of the growth may be undertaken. Biopsy for confirmation of the diagnosis or simple mastectomy in selected patients will both avoid serious functional disability and will be minimally deforming from a cosmetic standpoint. The therapeutic management can then appropriately focus on methods having a systemic effect, a response to which will influence the prognosis rather than the type of surgical attack on the primary site.

This approach would not impose an unacceptable burden on medical facilities. These very same diagnostic procedures are inevitably performed to determine the need for additional therapy but unfortunately *after* rather than *before* operations. At least the selected patient at higher risk of having the cancer lesion deserves a more reflective decision making to avoid being subjected to a radical mastectomy when it can be recognized that such a major operation has no potential for being curative. It is hoped that what appears obvious in concept may find its way into routine practice.

It is sad that Meg Land did not read what Dr. Johnson had to say, but Olivia Newman did. Or if she didn't she did not need to, for Olivia Newman's experience was the diametric opposite to Meg Land's. Meg's cancer treatment did not have to be so rushed— if only she had known she had a choice.

* It should be noted that currently the risk/benefit ratio of routine mammographic screening of asymptomatic (no apparent symptoms) women 35-50 is under debate. The National Cancer Institute/American Cancer Society has issued interim guidelines and plans to make an official statement in the near future. These interim guidelines are available on request from the American Cancer Society, 777 Third Avenue, New York, New York 10017

TWO
Olivia Newman

Slim, five-foot-six Olivia Newman is incandescent with energy. She is thirty-seven. High cheekbones offset an aquiline nose and green eyes. She has an easy, simple, and open personality. She has never been able to hide her emotions. An early marriage precluded college, but she is a bright and involved woman, particularly when it comes to the school activities of her three young sons. She and her husband, Clark, live in a modest home on a crowded hillside of look-alike tract homes. They live in Glendale, California, where Clark is the part-owner of a body repair shop and Olivia often helps with household expenses as a part-time secretary in an insurance company.

Olivia Newman and Meg Land would probably never meet, even should they live in the same city. The two are worlds apart socially and economically. But Olivia was no less aware of cancer campaigns than Meg. Since she technically lives in Los Angeles, she and her family have been interested in the lively and frequent recent efforts of local television and radio stations to run weekly series on breast cancer examination and cancer detection.

At first these programs about breast examination were scorned by Olivia's husband and he had serious doubts that their younger boys should watch them.

But Olivia was equally insistent that her husband and children watch. She was a woman who did not take the news of Mrs. Ford's or Mrs. Rockefeller's medical misfortunes lightly. It made sense to her that if the media were making an all-out effort to inform the public about breast cancer, it must be important. Clark said it was probably just another sensational media gesture, but there was one nagging matter that kept him watching and reading. It was that Olivia, his wife of seventeen years, examined her breasts each month. He remembered that Olivia had been practicing breast self-examination for over two years. He certainly could not remember anything traumatic that had taken place having to do with Olivia's breasts. She had been a fairly healthy woman—with the exceptions of her yearly bouts with bronchitis and the two times she had been hospitalized (besides the times that she had had her children) once for the removal of her appendix and once for a serious kidney infection.

Clark asked his wife about the reason for her concern in examining her breasts. Olivia replied that she had originally become interested when one of her son's teachers had had a mastectomy two years before. It was at about the same time that it was necessary for her to make an appointment to see her doctor for an annual checkup.

Olivia had always liked her doctor. She had never really thought about exactly why—she just did.

She had trusted him since the time Tommy had burst in the back door crying, "Mommy, Mommy, my hand!" Blood was streaming down his arm as he held it up to her. He had cut it on a broken bottle. There were spots of blood on his Batman T-shirt and blue jeans. For a moment, Olivia had panicked—Clark was gone—but then she remembered Dr. Stevens' office. She wrapped the hand in a towel and drove there. He had calmly washed and then sutured the child's cuts. After the blood was gone, they really didn't look so big, but Olivia would never forget that day and had remained loyal to him ever since.

Dr. Stevens was in his early fifties now. Short, slightly overweight, his ruddy complexion and thin gray hair made him no Robert Redford. Still, he smiled a lot and really did seem to listen and care.

A sign reading "Thomas K. Stevens, MD, Family Practice" hung outside the one-story stucco building in suburban Glendale that was his office. Olivia idly picked up a battered copy of *Time* from one of the chairs in the waiting room. In it she found yet another article on Mrs. Ford and her mastectomy. She chose to read the section on inflation instead, but found it boring. Soon it was her turn to go through the door by the nurse's desk and be led to the examining room. Her chart was already in the clip on the door.

After a few questions, Dr. Stevens began to examine her. As he examined her breasts, she suddenly felt compelled to ask him why he always examined her breasts when her gynecologist or internist never did so. At this moment the stage was being set for Olivia, the questioning and concerned patient. Her casual question was, however, asked so that no light answer could be given. Dr. Stevens was willing to take a great deal of time with his patients, when it would have been easier to give a brief and summary response. However, instead of answering Olivia directly, he asked her a question. "Olivia, do you examine your own breasts?"

"No, I don't—usually. I know I should, but I never seem to find the time. And when I do try, I'm not even sure what to look for. I've tried to imitate you a few times, but then I guess it was just really forgotten . . . I know I should."

Olivia was slightly flushed. She *did* know that she should examine her breasts. She'd read enough stories and seen enough ads run by the American Cancer Society in magazines with Sophia Loren telling the readers to "examine their breasts." She had even received Society literature in the mail.

Fortunately Olivia had asked why. And, fortunately, her doctor had not only spent the time to examine her breasts routinely each time she visited him, but now was willing to spend additional time to show her how to properly examine her own breasts.

He explained that the purpose of breast self-examination was simply to give her an earlier chance of detecting cancer. The idea was not to examine her breasts with an expectation of finding a lump but rather to think of the procedure as preventive medicine.

Olivia listened with amazement as he told her that one of every fourteen women born in the United States would develop breast cancer. He told her that breast cancer was a leading cause of death among women. Olivia had read these statistics many times before. She had thought about breast self-examination, but until this moment with her doctor, she had somehow dismissed it, forgotten about it, was usually too rushed to do anything about it. Suddenly everything had become real.

Olivia was now ready to learn how to examine her breasts properly. It would take a bit of practice to discover the lumps and bumps that were natural to her particular breasts, but Dr. Stevens explained that she knew her own body better than anyone else. It was simple mathematics, he said. If Olivia only saw him once a year, and she had been practicing monthly breast self-examination, she would be eleven times more experienced than he. Also, she was taking responsibility for her body, and she would have the advantage—perhaps—of making an early discovery of anything unusual that occurred visually or internally within her breast— any changes in the skin or nipple, any dimpling or puckering, any lumps—in fact, any abnormality whatever.

He could see that Olivia was listening, but she looked worried. "Listen, Olivia, there's nothing to get panicky about. I want to assure you of something very important. Seventy-five percent of all lumps biopsied in 1975 proved not to be cancer. Seventy-five percent, Olivia, and there were four hundred and fifty thousand biopsies performed this year in the United States. Women themselves discovered ninety percent of those lumps. Now, most were found accidentally by women when the lumps were big enough to feel. Sadly, only a few women practice breast self-examination."

Olivia could see his jaw set with anger. He went on.

"We had over ninety thousand cases of diagnosed cancer this

year alone. Somehow the message is not getting out to women that they themselves can do more to lower the death rate of cancer than anything medicine has to offer—more than any amount of surgery, radiation, chemotherapy, or anything else. If women could only understand that the chances for arresting a cancerous tumor become greater when it is discovered at its smallest possible detectable size. If only women could understand that, then perhaps they would realize that delaying a visit to a physician for even a month after the discovery of a lump could prove a fatal decision! I don't want to scare you. I want you to understand that I am trying to give you as much information as possible. I want you to understand that if you do find a lump in your breast, you must do something about it immediately. You know, a lot of women come in to see me with a lump that has been there for months—sometimes even years. It really makes me sad and angry. What it comes down to is this: *You* are the person who must be directly responsible for your own health."

Olivia was engrossed in what Dr. Stevens was saying to her. It made sense. She asked him why women waited so long. The doctor sighed, leaned back on his chrome stool, and reached up with his hand to rub the back of his neck.

"Well, Olivia, there's no simple answer. I would say fear is the number one deterrent to women visiting their doctors on discovery of a lump. Most women simply can't handle the fear of the possibility of a cancerous lump, the possibility of a mastectomy, and the possible alteration of their relationships with their husbands or boyfriends. Dr. Guy Robbins, a breast specialist, found that eighty percent of the women who enter the hospital for a biopsy 'feel' the result will be the loss of a breast.

"In reality, seventy-five percent of these lumps are benign, as I've told you before. The reason for delay is often economic. Particularly in these days of economic crisis, many patients of limited means worry about hospital costs and doctor's bills that may run into the hundreds or thousands of dollars. While many people have insurance, it's often insufficient to cover the total amount required for examination, mammograms, xerograms, thermograms, biopsy, or even surgery.

"You know, I've talked with many women who've delayed up to a period of several years before they could bring themselves to see a doctor about a lump. Since they felt well, and the lump didn't seem to change, they naively assumed that nothing was the matter. I'm appalled that American women, women with college degrees and even those with nursing degrees, continue to be astonishingly poorly informed. That this lack of information and common sense should exist in this country, with our sophistication in science, technology, and communication, is a disgrace."

Olivia was ruffled. She shot back an angry question. "Why should you put the blame solely on women?"

The doctor sat forward. "Look, Olivia, I don't. We in the medical profession are just as much responsible for the situation, if not more so, than women. Informing women is our responsibility, but the news just doesn't seem to get out fast enough." He stood up and pushed the chrome stool back into place. "Well, Olivia, those are some of the whys and hows women fail to examine their own breasts. But let's not dwell on that. Let's learn how to examine your breasts properly.

"Now, since you are still menstruating monthly, you are considered to be premenopausal. The time to examine your breasts is seven days after your menstruation has stopped. Many women pick any day during the month, but that's not the correct procedure since, as you know, your breasts go through many changes during the month, particularly when you're menstruating.

"For example, directly before your period begins, you may notice swelling or tenderness. There's a lot of activity going on. So it's very important that your self-examination be done seven days after your period, when the swelling that took place before your period is gone. Monthly breast examination is a simple, painless procedure that takes only a few minutes out of the day, and it could save your life. I often suggest that women commence their

Figure 4

Line rendering of the visual examination.

breast examination during their bath or shower by first observing their breasts while standing in front of the mirror."

He asked Olivia to remove her paper gown and step in front of the mirror above the washbasin. "The first part of examining your breasts is to look at them—this is called the visual exam.

"It is necessary to become very familiar with your breasts, Olivia. Notice that your left breast is a little larger and a little less geometrical than your right; this is very common, so it's nothing to worry about. To begin with, your arms should be kept at your sides, then lifted above the head."

Olivia raised her arms above her head. (See figure 4, page 75)

"That's fine. Now the reason for the lifting of the arms is that the stretching of the arms in an upward motion provides a tension on the skin of the breasts, making any abnormalities easier to see. It's important to look for any changes in the shape or size of the breasts, lifting or sinking of either nipple, or dimpling or puckering on the skin of the breasts, making any abnormalities easier to see. If you have any doubt at all, ever, about what you see in your breasts, you should call me immediately."

Having asked Olivia to lower her arms, he encouraged her, suggesting that she turn a little to observe each breast in the mirror.

Olivia was a bit surprised that Dr. Stevens was taking so much time with her. It was a unique experience.

"After you've thoroughly looked at your breasts, then it's time to feel them. An easy way to begin the manual part of a breast examination is while you're in the bath, when your skin is wet and slippery with soap. Your fingers slide easily over the breasts. Remember to keep the fingers flat, and to touch every part of the breast with the pads of the fingers. You know, a lot of women think it's sufficient to just sort of feel around the breast, and they are too rough with their breasts. Self-examination is a very gentle process. Now, give me your hand. Outstretch your hand. Good. Now, these are the pads of your fingers."

He pointed to the flat undersurfaces of her outstretched fingers. "The pads are your fingers' most sensitive part." (See figure 5,

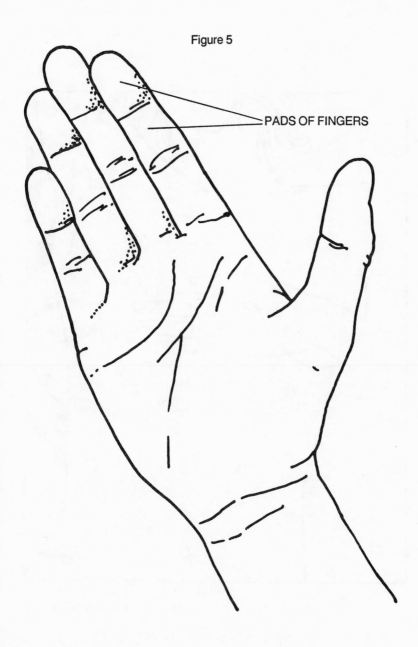

Figure 5

PADS OF FINGERS

Hand extended to show pads of fingers.

Figure 6

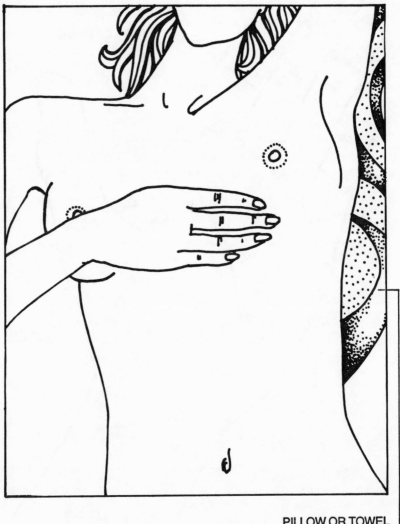

PILLOW OR TOWEL

Place a pillow or folded towel under the shoulder.

Figure 7

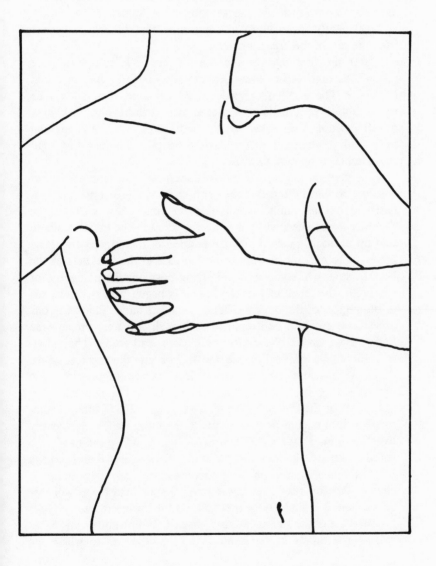

Do not grasp breast. Feel gently.

page 77) Olivia felt the undersurface of her left index finger. It did seem more sensitive than the tip of her finger.

"Feel gently for a lump or thickening that is clearly distinct from the rest of the breast tissue.

"After the first part of the manual check is completed, the more important step of breast examination is to lie flat on a bed or couch. The arm on the side to be examined first should be raised above your head and placed underneath your neck in a folded position." He asked Olivia to lie down on the examining table and produced a pillow, which he placed under her right shoulder. (See figure 6, page 78)

"The point to placing the pillow underneath the shoulder is that it serves to elevate the shoulder and shifts the breast so that it is flattened out as thinly as possible on your chest wall. If the shoulder is not elevated by a pillow or a towel, the breast tends to fold up on itself, making the examination of the larger part of the breast quite difficult because of an increase in the thickness of the breast. Now, while you're in this lying position, the palpation, or feeling, of the inner half of the breast is begun with the flat pads of the fingers of the opposite hand, your left hand. Think of your breast as a clock to be examined as though you were moving the fingers from twelve o'clock to one o'clock, and so on. The palpation should be gentle because the fingers are the most sensitive during very gentle touching. Don't just grasp your breast." (See figure 7, page 79). "Start from your nipple and work toward the outer part of the breast." (See figure 8, page 82). "I often recommend a little talcum powder to make the fingers glide more easily over the skin. That's right, now press lightly. Move the hand in a spiral, starting in a clockwise position." (See figures 8 and 9, page 83)." Palpate all the parts of the breast for any new lump or change. As you reach the lower part of your breast you will discover there is a slight ridge that follows the lower crescent of your breast. That is not an indication of disease. Women often make this ridge for a tumor. But if there is any question as to where the ridge is or what it should feel like, it is always best to have a doctor check it out to help you familiarize yourself with it. Of course, sometimes a lump can stand out from the ridge.

"It is most important to pay attention to the outer part of the breast, which is often the most difficult section to examine because it is the thickest. The reason it is so important is that malignant tumors are often discovered in that area. You must also extend your examination up underneath to the axilla, or armpit, and down the side near the outside of the breast to check for any lump in the lymph node area." (See figure 8, page 82). "After examination of one side has been completed, the exact reverse examination is done on the opposite breast.

"Okay, Olivia, shift your pillow underneath your left shoulder and fold your left arm underneath your neck."

Olivia began a systematic check of her left breast with her right hand, stopping now and again to ask questions about some of the things he had told her.

"All right, Olivia, now you can sit up. When you sit up, you can see that your breast become more pendulous, and it is therefore easier to feel the area around your nipple.

"When women can adhere to this routine of breast examination and become familiar with the physical characteristics of their breasts, there will be a much higher percentage of them who check with their physicians about any small lump that might develop."

The doctor asked Olivia to get dressed and then to join him in his office.

As she put on her clothes, she thought about the conversation. It was much easier to examine her breasts than she had imagined. She had read an article in a magazine with diagrams that made it look impossible.

She walked down the little hallway and through the open door into his office. He was sitting at a large desk, writing something on her chart. On the wall to his left were several framed documents,

Figure 8

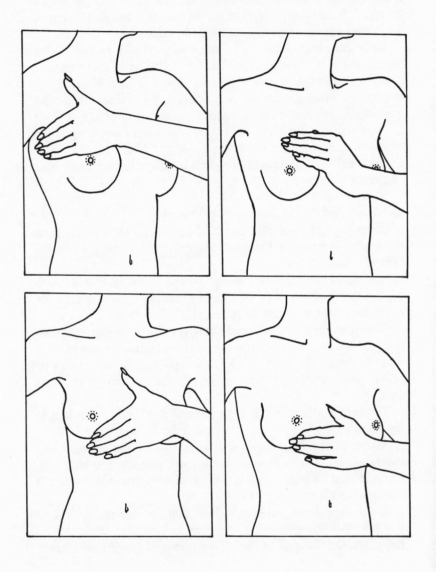

Feel under the arm (axilla) and around the breast like a clock.

Figure 9

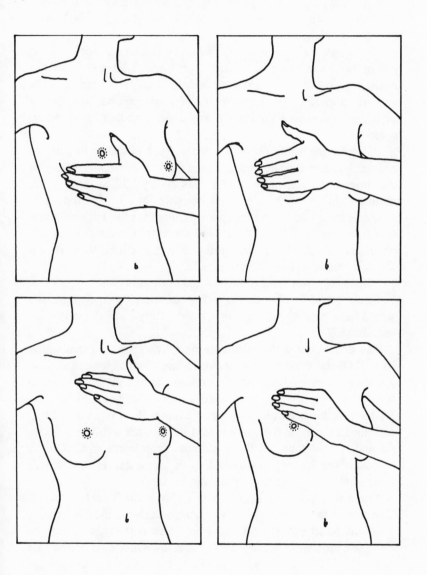

Touch gently. Work toward outer part of breast

a photo of his wife holding a marlin, and some shelves with books. Olivia sat down in a comfortable black swivel chair. He looked up from her chart.

"In going over your chart, I see that our office has not included you in the use of our breast exam chart insert. I already know the answers to most of these questions from today's session. There's one very important question here. Olivia, have you had any history of breast cancer in your family, any aunt, grandmother, mother, sisters?"

Olivia sat up in the chair. "Yes, my Aunt Margaret had breast cancer. I remember she had a mastectomy. I was really young at the time, and I remember that it was a very hushed matter. My mother didn't want to talk about her sister at all. My aunt came to see us from San Francisco about six months after her operation. Her right arm was very swollen and she wore some sort of elastic on it. Her clothes were very bulky. She didn't look well. It was about six months later that she died."

"Olivia, can you remember how old your aunt was?"

Olivia sat and reflected for a few minutes. "Yes, I think she would have been about forty-two, maybe forty-three, I really can't remember."

The doctor wrote this new data on Olivia's breast examination sheet. "Olivia, most doctors begin the use of what we call *screening mammography* with women around the age of thirty-three to forty; that is, when they enter into a group that has a higher risk for the possible occurrence of breast cancer. However, we feel that mammography or xerography should be initiated with any woman, no matter how young, if the physician is suspicious of a woman's breast. If she has any family history of breast cancer, a doctor is more likely to be suspicious about her breasts.

"I am sure you have heard about it, but it won't hurt to review. The reason that mammography and xerography is used is because they can detect abnormalities in your breast that neither I nor you can pick up simply by feeling the breast—abnormalities that are hidden, small and unsuspected. They work like an X-ray. And they simply show in detail the tissue structure of your breast. Mammography and xerography can pick up many benign things such as cystic disease, fibrosis, and fibroadenoma. More importantly, mammography and xerography can pick up the primary and secondary signs of cancer.

"Because of your age, Olivia, and the fact that your aunt had cancer, I would like to recommend that you have a xerographic examination."

Olivia was confused. "You seem to interchange mammography and xerography. Are they two different processes, and why have you chosen xerography for my examination?"

"Well, actually, xerography is very similar to mammography. However, there are some important differences. A mammogram is an X-ray of the breast that is developed on an X-ray film. It comes out black and white like an ordinary X-ray. A xerogram is also made by passing X-rays through the breast, but instead of an X-ray film, a plate similar to those used in a Xerox copier is exposed. From this plate, a blue-and-white picture is developed. It beautifully shows the details of the inside of the breast. Many of my colleagues feel that the detail obtained with the xerography procedure is significantly greater than that obtained through the conventional mammography. I agree with them. Also, xerography possibly gives a smaller radiation dose to the patient."

"Anyway, Olivia, I am going to send you over to the best radiologist I know. He comes highly recommended by other doctors, and both he and his technicians are involved in taking many mammograms and xerograms every day.

"Now, I'd like to make this important point. As any diagnostic tool, mammography or xerography can involve unavoidable errors. For example, errors can occur because of the position of the breast on the plate. So, obviously, the technicians involved in taking these films must be extremely well qualified. It is also critically important that the radiologist who reads the mammograms or xerograms be thoroughly familiar with all aspects, and not just some radiologist who sees only a few mammograms or xerograms a week. Interpreting them requires highly skilled and trained radiologists."

Interestingly enough, Dr. Stevens had taken a great deal of time with Olivia to explain as much as possible about breast self-examination, and has now suggested that she have a xerogram examination because of her age and the fact that her maternal aunt had had breast cancer, making her a higher-risk patient for this disease.

"Olivia, after my secretary has set up an appointment for you to have the xerogram examination, the technician from that radiologist's office will call you and give you more specific details. It's usually their practice to send out a small pamphlet about xerography along with some of the instructions they will want you to follow before the xerogram is done.

"Now, do you have any question at all about the technique of breast examination I have shown you?"

Olivia didn't, but she asked the doctor if he had any pamphlets or knew where she could get any literature to help her in her initial mastering of breast self-examination.

"Yes, I have a pamphlet put out by the American Cancer Society, and it is quite good. There's one point I want to emphasize. Because of your age and family history, you are in the higher-risk category, and I want you to be aware that your monthly breast self-examination is going to be an important part of your responsibility for your body and breasts. Also, I would like to set up a screening schedule so that we will make certain that you are checked biannually for a thorough breast examination, and a xerogram schedule will be set up depending on what we find in these first series you will complete. The rationale is simply this: The three parts of the woman's self-examination, the physician's biannual examination, and the use of mammography or xerography complement one another. They all work together. I can only do so much, however; it is up to you to maintain your schedule of monthly breast self-examination seven days after your period, make your own appointments, and so on.'

Dr. Stevens got up from his chair and came around the desk.

He opened the door for Olivia and walked with her through the hallway to the door leading to the receptionist's office. He was a busy man—no less so than other doctors—but he was able to find time in his schedule for thoughts about perspective and priorities. Olivia was lucky.

An Abnormal Xerogram

Having set up another breast examination six months hence, Olivia Newman left her doctor's office and returned home. Her boys were inhaling peanut butter and jelly sandwiches. Her husband arrived home at around four thirty. Olivia had no inhibitions or anxiety about showing him the pamphlet she had received from the doctor's office or about telling him about her experience. She told Clark how her doctor had taught her breast self-examination, and they read through the American Cancer Society pamphlet together without any sense of dealing with a mystical subject or, on his part, of invading exclusively female territory.

The phone rang: the technician at the radiologist's office was already calling to find out when it would be convenient for Olivia to come in for a routine mammographic examination, using the xerography technique. Having agreed on a time, the technologist mentioned she would be sending along a short pamphlet explaining how to prepare for the examination.

The next day a four-page pamphlet arrived in the mail and, although her doctor had explained how the process worked, the information was reinforced by the pamphlet. Once again, Olivia read that the majority of breast lumps are not malignant, and that in those few cases where cancer was detected, it was vital that it be detected as early as possible. She read that on the day of her examination, she was not to use any deodorant, perfume, powders, or creams in the underarm areas or on her breasts. The reason for this was that any residue of deodorants or creams on the skin could interfere with a clear xerogram. It was suggested that she wear a blouse with a skirt or slacks rather than a dress, since it was necessary to undress only to the waist for the examination.

Four days later, Olivia was sitting in the radiologist's reception room. While she was waiting, she filled out familiar forms about age, weight, and the name of her referring doctor. The technician summoning Olivia inside was businesslike and straightforward. "Mrs. Newman, I'd like you to remove all your clothing above the waist. Then we will be making some X rays of both your breasts since it is important to compare the images of each."

Olivia sat in a comfortable position in front of an adjustable flat X-ray table. The stool was also adjustable to account for her height. A procedure that began with her left breast was to be duplicated exactly with her right. First, her left breast was placed on an eight-by-ten film holder that rested on the table. She was told to use her left hand to press the edge of the film holder against her chest wall. Since the breast is a cone and not a hemisphere, a coned-shaped tube perpendicular to the floor was then brought over her shoulder. The point of the tube lay directly below her clavicle. The tube was pressed against Olivia to prevent motion. The technician used a spongelike object to aid in positioning Olivia's breast in order to minimize any air space between the film holder and the cone so that the clearest image could be made. Olivia was asked to sit, stand, or lie in various positions to obtain the X rays. After each film plate was exposed, Olivia's xerograms were immediately processed to make certain the images were sharp. Since they were, Olivia was free to leave. The entire examination had taken twenty-five minutes. From this point, the technician gave the xerograms to the radiologist. He studied and interpreted them and reported his findings to Olivia's physician. Within two days, Dr. Stevens called to tell her the xerograms were normal.

For the following eighteen months, Olivia Newman continued her biannual appointments with her physician for breast examination. And she made a conscientious effort to maintain a monthly schedule of breast self-examination. During that time, Olivia was to learn through her reading about other modes of breast examination, one of which was *thermography*. Thermography, she discovered, is used in the diagnosis of some breast disease because certain breast abnormalities produce a higher temperature than adjacent normal tissue. This technique reflects and focuses the heat emission from the breast and records it on a Polaroid film. Olivia had discussed this with her doctor, and he explained that he found the results of thermography inferior to xerography. He also explained that it really remained an experimental technique because it has not been perfected enough to accurately "pick-up" a cancer. Its results continue to provide a wrong indication more than 60 percent of the time. Therefore it should never be used alone as a diagnostic tool.

At the School of Public Health of the University of California, Berkeley, a breast check is being developed which would analyze breast fluid for cellular abnormality. Some recent findings show that all women have natural fluid in their breasts that can be extracted quickly (and painlessly) from the nipple. This can be done by applying direct pressure to the breast or by placing a small suction device over the nipple.

One test in particular may detect tumors long before they could be discovered by self-examination, X rays, or the recently developed thermography. This technique is thought to be a sort of breast Pap smear. That is, a way to check cells from the breast for signs of malignancy. Olivia had read in the newspaper that a study of this project had been launched at the Peralta Hospital in Oakland, California. The technique involved was simple. After the nipple was disinfected, some nipple or breast fluid was obtained and placed in a culture dish. The cells which developed in the dish were then subjected to detailed examination under light and electron microscopes. It was hoped that the cells demonstrating an ability to invade surrounding tissues would provide some clues regarding possible abnormal states. All this information was readily available for Olivia Newman to read, and since there had been so much publicity surrounding Mrs. Ford's and Mrs. Rockefeller's experiences with breast cancer, Olivia took an increasingly serious interest in finding out as much as she could about the disease. Many things she learned she found fascinating, even amazing.

Contrast mammoraphy is a new and experimental form of cancer detection. Tiny nylon catheters, in other words tiny tubes, are inserted into the duct openings around the nipple (using a microscope for exact placement). A water-based dye that shows up on X rays is introduced into the catheters which plug the breast. Then a mammogram is taken. With this mammogram, doctors can study the pattern of the breast ducts. Some researchers feel by using this technique on an abnormal breast, evaluation may be obtained without the need for a biopsy. Olivia had picked up a copy of a popular women's magazine and found that contrast mammography had been in use for some years in Santa Barbara, California, by Dr. Otto Sartorius. He introduced a water-based dye into the breast and then X-rayed the breast. When she asked Dr. Stevens about it, he explained that it was indeed quite experimental.

By this time Olivia was both sufficiently interested and involved to attend a women's lecture about breast cancer one evening, presented by Dr. Melvin Silverstein from the City of Hope Cancer Center. There she relearned the difference in the modes of breast examination, and that the most pressing problem in the treatment of breast cancer today is the inability of the physician to determine the extent of the cancer. More than half the women with operable breast cancer ultimately die of cancer that was present in their bodies but not found before the original procedure.

Olivia was cheered to hear that the future cancer-detection methods would come, hopefully, as new nuclear medicine techniques were improved to locate smaller areas of cancer in the body.

Olivia read in the Sunday paper of a study that the National Cancer Institute had supported. It reported that the combination of physical examination and X-ray mammography in breast cancer screening had been shown to decrease death owing to this disease. A group of 31,000 women screened for breast cancer by a New York health insurance plan had a one-third reduction in breast cancer deaths over a five-year follow-up. This was compared with a control group of 31,000 women given their usual medical care in their usual medical groups. The purpose of this program was early detection. One-third, 44 out of 132 of the breast cancers detected in the screening program, were found in X-ray mammography before the tumors were large enough to be detected physically. Only one of these 44 women died of breast cancer during the five-year period, indicating that early detection led to subsequently more effective treatment.

Women's magazines, television, and *Consumer Reports* were all discussing the matter of breast cancer detection. Self-examination, mammography, xerography, thermography, and dozens of experimental techniques were constantly being explored in detection and research centers. Olivia and her husband were also to learn that *there was no known sure cure for breast cancer. And they became aware of the battle and controversy raging thoughout the medical communities and research centers in the United States about the treatment of breast cancer. It sprang from the fact that the overall survival rate has not improved in the last twenty-five years, apparently regardless of how breast cancer has been treated.*

Most physicians, and even the American Cancer Society, still traditionally incline toward more radical procedures. However, the Newmans learned there were many different combinations of treatments that involve surgery, radiation therapy, chemotherapy, and immunotherapy. They noted that all of the studies were in their infancy and that breast cancer treatment and survival rates were enigmatic to the medical profession.

Perhaps one of the most important things Olivia discovered was that she would have *the right of participation in her choice of treatment,* if she had ever had the misfortune of developing breast cancer.

Many people, even medical professionals, are not aware of some new modes of treatment. Even if they are, what each treatment entails can be confusing to a woman when learned verbally from a surgeon during a single office visit. It could prove too much to understand and digest at one sitting. Particularly difficult is the situation in which the surgeon discusses the different forms of treatment while the woman is under the immediate stress of facing the possibility of having breast cancer.

In a report given by Dr. Max Cutler, director of the Beverly Hills Cancer Foundation, an important point concerning women's choice of treatment had been made. He said, "There remains a serious problem that demands attention. I refer to the woman who finds it impossible to face the emotional trauma of mastectomy. How far should a surgeon go in pressuring a patient into the larger operation? All of us who have dealt with this problem know there are certain women whose personal and emotional problems are such that they cannot easily accept mastectomy without risking serious and possibly irreparable psychological damage. In these circumstances, severe postoperative depression can become a serious problem that can lead to attempted suicide. . . . The responsibility of the surgeon in presenting the delicate problem of treatment to the patient is indeed great and calls upon the highest skills in the difficult art of the practice of medicine. . . ."

It occurred to Olivia that if she should perhaps become one of the 90,000 women each year who develop cancer of the breast, she could not possibly make a choice of treatment without adequate information. It also occurred to her that the choice of treatment could only effectively be used if she had time—*time for reflection between the biopsy and the treatment.* She discovered to her shock, by talking with friends and physicians, and by reading, that most women were never allowed time between biopsy and, if a diagnosis of cancer was found, a choice of treatment.

Olivia became alarmed and discussed her apprehensions with her husband. She made him promise that if she were ever in the position of having to have a biopsy—even though she knew that three-quarters of the biopsies performed did not indicate cancer— he would support her in making an informed choice if the physician diagnosed breast cancer. He agreed.

Olivia realized that the choice of treatment could only effectively be put to use if she requested what was known as a "two-step procedure." This simply meant that the standard method of admitting a woman to the hospital for a biopsy and possible immediate surgical treatment of diagnosed cancer would be broken into two parts, unless otherwise medically or psychologically indicated. First, the biopsy would be performed, the woman sent home, and the results from a thorough pathology study evaluated. If the biopsy specimen, after careful study, proved to be malignant, then the woman and her husband, or someone close to her, would confer with the surgeon. And this conference would take place *after* the woman had received a battery of tests—bone scans, liver scans, chest X-rays, and blood tests—to see if the cancer had spread to other parts of her body. This was called the "metastatic workup." It was then and only then that the choice of treatment could be decided upon. If advanced cancer was present in the body, small, less-deforming surgery was in order. Often chemotherapy was administered to the patient in an attempt to attack the widespread cancer in the body.

She also learned that there is growing evidence that a brief delay of a few days or more between the diagnosis of breast cancer and the treatment for it will not adversely affect the patient's survival chances. Current thinking on this problem from many different sources is summed up by Dr. Henry P. Leis, Jr., in his book *Diagnosis and Treatment of Breast Lesions*. As he and others have pointed out, the average breast cancer has been present in a woman's breast for six to eight years before it reaches the palpable size of one centimeter. It doubles at the average rate of about every one hundred days. Dr. Leis says, "It is hard, therefore, to understand the dramatic immediate surgery practiced by some surgeons on breast lumps without proper preparation. Certainly nobody can seriously consider that a delay of even a few weeks would make a difference in five-year survival rates. Proper preparation will reduce infection and allow the surgeon to know if the patient has any medical contraindications to his planned surgical procedure and whether there is any laboratory or X-ray evidence of distant metastasis."

Many times women are told by their surgeons, "If I find cancer at the time of biopsy, I'll have to do a mastectomy immediately. Otherwise the cancer will spread and you will surely die." Under the cloud of this very frightening pronouncement, most women agree to undergo the "one-step procedure." To Olivia's amazement, she discovered that the belief that surgery must be done immediately simply is not always valid in light of current medical knowledge. (See the Appendix, page 197, for a longer discussion of the evidence that delay between biopsy and surgery is safe.) Olivia wondered, "Why in the world do many surgeons continue to insist that it's not safe to wait a few days?" She was forced to conclude that (1) the doctors hadn't been reading their journals and were unaware that the relative safety of delay had been proven for many years, or (2) they read the data but chose to disregard it entirely, or (3) they were lying to their patients and themselves, or worse (4) they didn't want to include their patients in making a choice.

A one-step procedure was Meg Land's experience—it meant that the woman would sign an operation permit, before surgery, which allowed the surgeon to make all decisions at the time of the biopsy, based on what was earlier described as a quick-frozen pathology report, which is sometimes a suboptimal total diagnostic method. Obviously there is no way for the woman to know her ultimate outcome until after surgery.

Most surgeons do not practice the two-step procedure and many women do not know that it is possible to request a break in time between a biopsy and treatment.

A woman may often have to search for a surgeon who will agree to the two-step procedure. *She may have to modify the hospital form that gives consent for surgery by putting in her own handwriting that she will only allow a biopsy to be performed and nothing more—that no further surgical procedures may be carried out at that time.*

Since Olivia was also aware of the psychological aspects of breast cancer, she began to understand deep within herself that if she ever had to have a breast biopsy the two-step procedure would be the best manner for her to proceed. She realized that she would not feel driven to her emotional limits if she had only the biopsy to deal with. In contrast, Olivia thought that having to deal at the same time with both the biopsy and the possible removal of a breast without her knowledge would be psychologically overwhelming for her.

Olivia began to realize how fortunate she was to have had the initial contact with Dr. Stevens. She learned in talking with other women that most of their doctors did not spend much time with them at all. When Olivia attempted to share with other women her experiences and the knowledge she had gained, she discovered two things. First, few of the women had had regular breast examinations performed by their doctors, nor had they been practicing breast self-examination. Second, the women who had asked their doctors for information often found them unwilling to talk about the two-step procedure, in the event that biopsies became necessary. Some women even found themselves recipients of verbal attacks by their doctors. The attacks came in terms of the physicians' asserting that their patients were speaking from ignorance and that doctors always knew best. This kind of attack was frightening, since the women were faced with a dilemma. Historically, patients have always left things in the hands of their doctors. They have always thought, "The doctor knows best." One of Olivia's friends had to have a biopsy, and when her surgeon was presented with the idea of a two-step procedure, he produced a written contract for the woman to read that clearly stated things went his way or no way at all. Fortunately the woman had a negative biopsy. It was clear to Olivia that such a dictatorial attitude on the part of a doctor would be both frightening and depressing. Olivia sensed that her friend's doctor was threatening to abandon his patient at a time when she needed him most. Of course, that doctor got his way, for this was a strong but subtle form of medical blackmail. Olivia decided she would never submit to that kind of blackmail.

How can doctors feel outraged that women say, in fact, that they want to be in charge of their own bodies? That they want to be part of a decision-making process and have a voice in decisions concerning possible treatment they may receive? It was clear to Olivia that a woman should be able to speak with her doctor first at length and that, if a woman had to be admitted to a hospital for a biopsy, she should have all the kind, warm assurance and support necessary, as well. She should be allowed to participate in her own destiny.

For Olivia and her family, the days and nights went by in the usual pattern. The children were sent off to school, Little League games were attended, and on occasion Olivia would do some secretarial work.

She had been practicing breast self-examination monthly, and hadn't discovered anything at all unusual. She received a card in the mail from Dr. Stevens, reminding her it was time for his bi-annual breast examination. The card also mentioned he would like her to have a new set of xerograms made before he saw her for an examination. This she did. She visited the doctor's office and was examined. Afterward, Dr. Stevens asked Olivia to have a discussion with him in his office. Before him on his desk was her chart and the several sets of xerograms performed in the past, as well as the new ones. Olivia sensed a strange quietness in the room.

Dr. Stevens sat forward and asked Olivia to come around to the back of his desk. "Olivia, I want to show you something. Here are yesterday's xerograms from the radiologist along with his report. There seems to be some abnormality here in the right breast."

He spread the xerograms out on his desk. "I want you to look at the xerogram. You see, there are some slight changes that have taken place over the months. I am highly suspicious of this area in the upper quadrant of your right breast. You can see, here on the xerogram, a slight irregular shadow and some increased vascular supply to the breast. I'd like you to have a biopsy. I couldn't feel anything when I examined your breast today, but the radiologist's report indicated he felt a biopsy would be advisable. As you can see from your past xerograms, that shadow has been changing and becoming more defined."

Olivia looked slightly stunned. The doctor spoke again. "Remember, Olivia, three out of four biopsies are not cancer. I'd like to recommend you to a good surgeon whose specialty is breast surgery. You're lucky we have a breast specialist in this city. Ideally, a woman should see a specialist, but that's almost impossible for most women in the country. The majority find themselves in the hands of surgeons who only handle a few breast cases a month. It simply can't be avoided. If a woman can travel to a center it would be best for her, but time and money often make that impossible. The alternative is to have the general surgeon confer with a center by phone—at least the woman would be assured of having an expert 'in the case.' You can imagine how that idea might upset many surgeons. But they should understand that the woman and her needs come first!"

Many women had heard these very words from their doctors, but where they were usually fraught with emotion and anxiety, Olivia's natural anxiety was allayed by the security she had already been building as a bulwark against this day. She sat down.

"Dr. Stevens, will this surgeon perform a biopsy only?"

"Well, he generally does so unless his patients are against it, or unless he feels there is some reason not to. You'd probably like to discuss it with him."

The doctor called the breast surgeon personally while Olivia was in his office so she could overhear the conversation between the two physicians. An appointment was set up for Olivia and her husband.

When Clark came home from work that night, Olivia asked to speak with him privately in the bedroom. She explained what had happened and what they might face as a result. She told him about the suspicious discovery and the xerogram, and she told him calmly that an appointment had been set up for them with a surgeon.

One Step at a Time

Clark Newman understood what he could contribute to Olivia's sense of well-being at this moment. He took her in his arms and hugged her. She asked him quietly, "Will you come with me when I see the surgeon?" Like most men, Clark was not sure exactly what all this meant. It had been over a year since he had read the pamphlet Olivia had brought home from Dr. Stevens' office. He had seen his wife examine her breasts, and because of Olivia's insistence he had also watched the television programs on breast cancer. Still, this had only slightly prepared him for the reality that his wife was about to see a surgeon to check the possibility that she might have cancer. He only knew that she needed his help and support.

Olivia had made her husband promise some time ago that he would help her make it clear to the surgeon that he was to be allowed to perform the biopsy only. Together they discussed in greater detail the "what ifs." Clark asked Olivia if she were frightened.

"I'm not so much frightened as apprehensive," she said. But two thoughts kept going through her mind: "If it's cancer, how long do I have between the biopsy and the treatment?" and, "If it's cancer, what treatment am I going to select?" She said, "I still don't understand it all."

Her husband's well-meaning but inadequate assurance was that he was sure everything would work out all right.

It was on an unusually crisp and sunny California morning that Olivia Newman readied her children for school and finally got them all out the door. She and Clark left the house fifteen minutes later on their way to Dr. Emick's office.

Figure 10

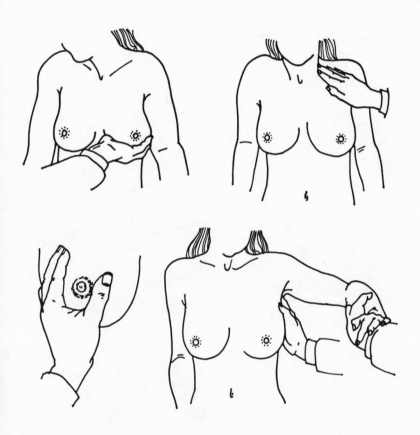

The doctor's examination.
A proper examination by your doctor should look like this.

Figure 11

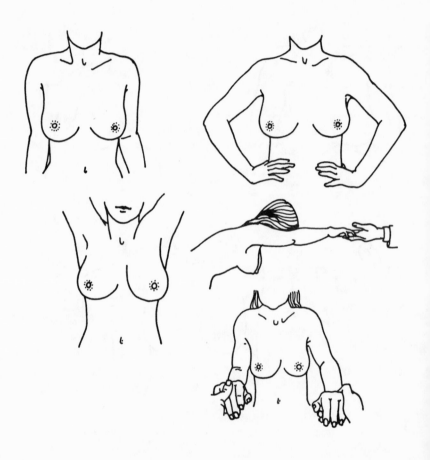

The doctor's examination.

Figure 12

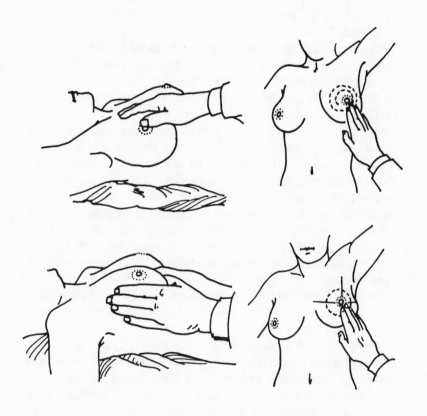

The doctor's examination.

There, more medical information cards were filled out and returned to the reception desk. As she was returning the cards to the receptionist, Olivia said, "After the doctor has completed my examination, I would like my husband to join me when I have a discussion with him." The receptionist smiled and replied, "Oh, yes, your family doctor already arranged for both of you to see Dr. Emick."

Olivia was called in for the breast examination. She undressed and put on the familiar paper gown. The doctor came into the examining room and introduced himself.

"I'm Dr. Emick," he said in a soft Southern drawl. He was in his mid-forties, about six feet tall, with longish brown hair. Under his white coat he wore a blue open-collar sports shirt. "I understand, Mrs. Newman, we have some xerograms here that are a little abnormal, so I would like to examine your breasts today. First, would you please lie down on the examining table?"

The examination was very thorough, thought Olivia. It seemed as though the surgeon was meditating over not only the suspicious right breast, but her normal breast as well. It lasted approximately twenty minutes, during which the surgeon asked her to sit up, lean forward, raise her arms above her head, while he completed the examination.

Dr. Emick told her that a thorough breast examination by a doctor should be carefully made. (See figures 10, 11 and 12, pages 99, 100, and 101.)

Olivia was a little surprised that this man was a surgeon. She thought surgeons were men who spoke little and acted rapidly and decisively, occasionally uttering some profound statements on life or death. Dr. Emick wasn't like that at all. He seemed like a warm, caring person. He definitely gave the feeling that he was willing to take plenty of time with her.

Afterward, Olivia went to the door of the reception room and asked her husband to join her in the doctor's office. She was not alone as many women are when they see their doctors. Dr. Emick felt it was extremely important to include the husband or whoever was closest to the patient when speaking with her. It gave him a chance to assess the woman's personal background and might offer an indication of what emotional and intellectual resources the woman in each instance had within her. He rarely sat behind his desk, but preferred instead to have close contact with his patients in order to attempt to break down the barrier of fears he knew many of them had inevitably constructed. In the quiet office, as Clark and Olivia sat close together, Dr. Emick carefully explained that he felt a biopsy was definitely necessary. This was based on Olivia's recent xerograms, which in comparison to her past xerograms now showed a shadow that might indicate cancer. Her family history of breast cancer made him even more suspicious.

In his soothing Kentucky drawl he began to explain more about the biopsy. "Mrs. Newman, the major purpose of a breast biopsy is either to prove the existence of or to exclude the possibility of cancer. You have been told that seventy-five percent of these biopsies are benign. Because of that high rate of nonmalignancy of breast tumors, I'd like to use the technique called a 'local biopsy.' This spares my patients any unnecessary exposure to a general anesthesia."

Olivia asked the doctor what it entailed.

"Essentially, Mrs. Newman, it means giving you a shot that will relax you, taking you to a small surgical room, and injecting your breast with a numbing agent much like the Novocain your dentist uses when you go to his office, and then biopsying the suspected area."

Olivia asked him why he used this particular biopsy method.

"Some time ago I asked myself why it is was necessary to perform breast biopsies on an inpatient basis—why subject all women to the grim details and time-consuming explanations of what might be done if a malignant tumor is discovered while a patient is under a general anesthesia?

"Now I suspect that you are aware that many women have delayed a significant period of time upon discovery of a lump before visiting their physicians for examinations. They are deathly afraid that they may go into a hospital for a breast biopsy and awaken without a breast, and so they refuse to acknowledge the lump's existence. Even apart from that, we know three-quarters of these biopsies are going to be benign. So I asked myself why must the woman experience that kind of mental trauma? There's no need to discuss the possibility of cancer and mastectomy if she is just being admitted for a biopsy. We have found in our hospital and elsewhere that the patient's fears and anxieties are heightened by the fact that she is requested to sign a permission form for a possible mastectomy.

"The two factors—one, discussing the possibility of malignancy, and, two, signing a permission form for a procedure that could take place while the patient is asleep—often erase in her mind any of the doctor's assurances that she might have a noncancerous lump.

"On the other hand, if a woman knows she is coming into a hospital for a biopsy only, her mental anguish is considerably reduced. Patients who are aware of what is going on, and know that they only face a biopsy, are far less frightened. Furthermore, if the biopsy is done with a local anesthetic, the woman has only to deal with the biopsy emotionally. She does not have to deal with the possibility of waking up without a breast. As I mentioned before, Mr. and Mrs. Newman, the procedure itself is a very simple one. Mrs. Newman will receive a premedication injection that will relax her, and a small amount of local anesthetic will be injected into the breast to deaden the area. The lump, or suspicious tissue, will be excised, the wound sutured closed, and then she will be free to return home after a few hours, during which she will very probably sleep off the medication."

He had looked at them carefully from time to time to see if they understood what he was saying. Olivia thought his words were well chosen and that he seemed a practical and down-to-earth person. Then he said, "The tissue that is taken from the breast is sent to the pathologist for what we call a 'permanent-section examination.' "

At this point Dr. Emick took an unusual course—he told Olivia about a procedure briefly referred to earlier in this book, one used in shockingly few cases but one he felt was necessary.

"In over ninety percent of the cases of breast biopsies in this country, a frozen-section diagnosis is used. The important difference is this: The frozen pathology report takes about fifteen to twenty minutes to complete. Although these diagnoses are usually correct, there have been some tragic mistakes made. I'm personally aware of several instances in which this frozen-section method of examining the tissue from a biopsy was diagnosed as cancer. The twenty-four-hour-or-more permanent pathology report proved the issue not to be cancerous. So, meanwhile, the woman lost her breast for benign disease. In other words, those women did not have cancer, and their diagnosis was based solely on a fifteen-minute frozen-section pathology report.

"You know, Mrs. Newman, it is possible to speculate about the national incidence of such tragedies. They could certainly have been avoided by using the local biopsy technique."

But Olivia was still confused about the differences in the two techniques. So was her husband. Dr. Emick said, "I can understand your questions. I've talked a lot this morning. Let me explain a little more.

"By using the local biopsy technique, the surgeon and the pathologist have the permanent section examined and diagnosed *before* proceeding to any further surgery. Now, as I told you, the frozen-section pathology report takes some twenty minutes. The permanent process is quite different. The tissue is first fixed in formaldehyde for from three to twelve hours. In this process, the tissue is then put through a time-consuming, multistage procedure that is highly complicated and that gives a high-quality, very definitive slide. The advantages of this method are many: the fix is better, the tissue shrinkage more uniform, the whole process is slower, and therefore it reduces tearing of the tissue and distortion of its structure. The tissue cuts thinner and thinner in this manner. The method of fixation allows tissue to take up the stain better than the frozen section. Also, the pathologist has the whole tissue block available for cutting samples at a later date. The definition and character of a single cell is much clearer and more precise than in a frozen section; thus, the pathologist has better tissue to work with. Also, if it is cancer, I'll know exactly what type it is and how serious it is."

Olivia asked why he was spending so much time on this topic. "Well, I feel that it's very important. I work very closely with my surgical pathologist concerning every case. We both feel it is imperative. The pathologist is a doctor, too, you know—he is not just a microscope. So I give the clinical information of a patient's history to the pathologist, and when dealing with a breast biopsy, this is especially important. Some of the clinical information of utmost importance is: the age of a patient, if she is postmenopausal or premenopausal, when her last menstrual period was, if she is taking medication, particularly any hormones, and so on.

"Bear with me, since you should know as much as possible about how the fate of your own body is decided. In sixty-five to seventy percent of the cases, in-depth clinical history is not of great importance; in over a quarter of the cases, the history and physical findings will be of the greatest assistance in making a diagnosis. This, of course, only has to confirm a diagnosis. When the pathologist and a surgeon look at a tissue section, they first look at the tissue and then at the history, in order to remove all bias from the opinion of their diagnosis. You should know this, too: *If the diagnosis is malignant, I will often send the slides to another pathologist without including the conclusions of the first. That gives me a second, uninfluenced decision.* Also, if there should be a diagnosis of cancer, you can request that your slides be sent to a consulting pathologist at another center. It really is the same good practice as always asking for a second opinion, from a doctor of your choice, any time surgery or treatment is involved.

"If you are uncomfortable with the thought of having your lump excised with this type of local biopsy, then—although I really don't like to do it that way—I could administer a general anesthetic. You already know that I won't be performing any definitive surgical treatment right away, so giving you a general anesthetic during the biopsy would mean subjecting you to two general anesthetics if the pathology report indicates you have cancer and require any surgery. There are other reasons why I usually won't perform any definitive treatment at the time of biopsy, but I would prefer to go into that subject at a later time. *Some surgeons feel that this method of biopsy is wrong. They still feel that if there is cancer in the breast, any delay in surgery would allow the cancer to spread. There are two camps of thinking, and some camps who don't think—they just keep performing the same surgery all the time without question. I only think it's fair to mention that there are some surgeons who feel differently.* it. *You are the one who is having the biopsy, and you come first. Stevens, can give you some other surgeon's name if you would like it. You are the one who is having the biopsy, and you come first.* Right now I'm concerned about how *you* feel about this type of biopsy. I don't want to push anything on you. It's your decision."

Olivia was obviously a great deal happier—and relieved—by the surgeon's openness. "I think I'd prefer the local biopsy. How long do I have to stay in the hospital?"

"It's just a day's stay. You should understand, though, that there are some cases when I would *not* use this method of biopsy. Sometimes a lump is very large or very deep. Then, too, many women just don't want to know what's going on. But there are many advantages to the local biopsy. In this city it's easier to find operating time for a minor than a major surgery. Using minor surgical facilities is considerably less expensive than tying up an entire operating room, anesthesiologists, and nurses—not to mention the extra days spent in the hospital. With today's increasing shortage of hospital beds, it's important to look at the economic aspect also."

Olivia looked at her husband. The mention of money meant a lot to them. The doctor went on.

"Our hospital is one of the few using the outpatient procedure of biopsy first and, if necessary, treatment second, There are a variety of other reasons for that approach, but they lie way beyond the biopsy. *Right now, Olivia, let's work with the biopsy first—one step at a time.*

"Do not eat or drink anything after Thursday midnight. Check into the hospital Friday morning at eight.

"Likely there will be some other women on your ward who will be there for the same reason you are. The hospital staff has set up an educational biopsy discussion session, meant to give you as much information as possible about the procedure—how it's done, and so on. Also, Mr. Newman, there will be a few husbands in the group you will be meeting. There will also be a social worker experienced in this area to answer any questions you or the other husbands might have, and also to give you all of the details available."

The surgeon rose from his desk. "We all want to make this as easy as possible for both of you."

Olivia's admission to the hospital was set for Friday morning.

Although she was slightly tense, the fact that she had to cope only with the local biopsy eased that tension. She also had some time to adjust to the thought of the biopsy and to think about any further questions she wanted answered. Because of her own knowledge, and the openness of her surgeon, which put her at ease, she felt prepared to deal with what was coming.

Friday morning arrived. Clark drove Olivia to the hospital. There was not exactly a lightness between them, but there was communication. Each was aware that they were both involved in what was about to take place.

Olivia was greeted warmly by the head nurse when she arrived on the ward. She was given a surgical consent form to read and sign. It was short, clear, and in large type. A blank space had been filled in with the words, "Right breast biopsy only—local aneshetic." That was the extent of the surgery Olivia would be having that Friday morning. Within moments of her arrival in her room, a technician appeared to take a blood sample and a urine specimen for the minor surgery. Meanwhile, Clark was escorted to a waiting area. He had visited with her briefly, until it was time to prepare for her biopsy. He joined the other husbands, who were in the hospital discussion group for men.

Olivia was in a hospital room with four other women. She pulled the drapes around her bed and changed into a hospital gown, robe, and slippers. A nurse opened one of the curtains slightly and asked, "Mrs. Newman, would you care to join us for the discussion group on what is going to take place this morning?"

The day after her biopsy, Olivia explained to a neighbor from the discussion group.

"Although I was nervous, I was glad I could participate. It was different from the way things had been handled with some of my friends.

"I knew the usual procedure was that a woman enters the hospital for a breast biopsy and receives a general anesthetic, with no psychological support or preparation for the possibility of losing a part of her body. The chance to participate in a more sensitive, supportive approach to a breast biopsy was really an important step, and there were other women in the group who clearly felt the same way. The purpose was to help us all to prepare our minds and bodies for something of major importance that most women face alone.

"I remember the eyes of the social worker as they swept our circle of five. She wasn't going to miss anything. The head nurse who had greeted me at the desk was patting the hand of an older woman. I was glad to see the young nurse, whom I recognized from the surgeon's office."

The neighbor asked, "Weren't you self-conscious?"

"A little," Olivia replied.

"The social worker started off by asking if anyone in the group had had a breast biopsy before. A twenty-year-old girl named Cindy laughed self-consciously. 'Oh, yes, eight months ago I had one done back in Kansas.'

"That got everyone's attention. She was really a veteran in our small ranks—and she was so young! She said that the other doctors had put her to sleep, which 'freaked her out' because she knew she would wake up without a breast at twenty. She talked about how grateful she was to her doctor and the hospital for permitting her to have a local biopsy—'It will be a comfort to know what's being done to my body.' And, more importantly, she felt that even if the lump proved cancerous, she wanted the option of considering various kinds of treatment.

"Cindy's positive attitude seemed to unify our group. In turn, I think she felt our admiration and our intent to emulate her example of rational openness—young people are so open these days. Each woman in her own way said how relieved she was to know she would not have to have a general anesthetic. The fear of awakening to the nightmare of a severed breast no longer haunted any of us. When the nurse asked how we had originally discovered our lumps, a woman named Cara spoke first. She said she felt something hard and raised on her left breast while showering. She said she wasn't worried, but I could tell that she must have been really frightened at the time. Cara was young, maybe thirty. She was Spanish-American and devastatingly beautiful. I could see how nervous she was. I think we all communicated some reassurance to Cara and she seemed to relax. At least, later on she had a genuine smile.

"A woman named Martha, who was about fifty, revealed that her concern was not so much for herself as for her six children. She said that she had been away from her family before, but that *this* time it was different! Martha seemed an ideal mother to me," Olivia continued. "She put her hand on her left breast, then she softly told us how she had discovered something hard there. To see if it could be her imagination, she had asked her husband to feel one breast, then the other. He could feel it, too. Well, there she was with us, and she wanted it to be over so she could return to her family that evening. Cara really helped when she gently held Martha's hand and told her it would be all right, that we would all be together—and we would be in our homes that night.

"When the head nurse asked a young woman named Debbie about her lump, she told us she had been aware of it *for two and a half years!* If her new boyfriend hadn't insisted she come in to be checked, she wouldn't have been there at all. As far as she was concerned, if it did mean cancer, she didn't want to know about it. We were all nonplussed by her curious logic," Olivia remembered, "but nevertheless Debbie said as long as she was there, it helped a lot to know she would have the biopsy this way. She said she didn't want those doctors doing anything to her that she didn't know about! Debbie's reasoning reminded me that no matter how trying the uncertainty was, we were all doing the right thing—we were actively investing in better health.

"Then, so that we all would know what to expect, the social worker and the head nurse gave a detailed account of the procedure. Dr. Emick, whom all of us had already met, would visit after the discussion group to chat and answer questions. All of us had to remove any nail polish or jewelry and take a shower before the minor surgery. The head nurse explained that we would get an injection that would relax us and make us slightly drowsy. However, she said, some of us would sleep, some would be drowsy, but we would all be awake enough to be able to speak. She asked again if anyone had had anything to eat or drink since midnight. She mentioned that a cloth screen would be placed between our neck and head in the operating room.

"The nurse also told us that we would receive an injection of Xylocaine to numb the area of the breast, almost like the one the dentist administers before he starts his work. After that the surgeon would do the biopsy. And after the procedure was complete, she told us he would apply an elastic pressure bandage on our breast. The nurse said that it would slightly flatten out our breast and would be much larger than the actual incision. She told us not to worry—the breast would be all there—it was just a removal of the lump and some tissue around it. If the tissue appeared to be suspicious, Dr. Emick would let us know at once, although the final pathology report would take a few more days. The pathology report was the final answer. Then she said we'd most probably sleep for part of the day until discharged in the early afternoon. The nurse wanted to make everything as easy as possible for us all in every way. She even told us not to be afraid of the doctor—that he was a person who cared a great deal about his patients. We could feel free to ask him anything we wanted! The frightening unknown had been chartered for us in detail. The discussion caused my fear almost to vanish. Then all of us began to talk more openly about our individual feelings, and we continued after the staff had left. We all knew we had one another.

"I remember the sense that there was a common thread uniting us all. The biopsy.

"We all asked the same question at the beginning of the session: 'Why me?' There were no rational answers that could be given at that time, but the second question was more concrete. Everyone wanted to make sure they were going to have the biopsy alone. The head nurse and the social worker assured us. The anxiety and psychological stress present when we first arrived at the hospital had largely been relieved. We were women sharing a common problem. We could reach out to one another and see that we were not alone. The idea of being together made the whole experience far easier for me.

"It was very exciting—inspiring, really—to watch ourselves move beyond ourselves, out toward a stranger—in spite of some still lingering personal anxieties.

"We all felt that there was another woman whose problems seemed greater . . . the older woman, the Chicana girl, the angry young woman, and myself. . . . We all learned from one another, leaned on one another, and perhaps even expanded our capacity to care about a stranger.

"Although it was obvious some of the women adapted to the stress better than others, we all had a very definite advantage, belonging to the group discussion. We knew that we had the support and concern of our surgeon, the nurses, the social workers, and one another. The path didn't seem so desolate.

"I had been tremendously impressed with the group discussion we had, particularly since it seemed to lessen the anxiety that we all felt," Olivia continued. "It let us open ourselves and discuss our fears of possible cancer and breast loss. We were grateful that we had the opportunity to fully discuss the event *before* it happened. I still felt awkward, and anxious, but I was united with four other women—previously strangers—with whom I would face a shared major event, a breast biopsy.

"Then Dr. Emick came to visit each one of us individually. He tried to tell us as much as possible about what was going to happen during the biopsy. And all of this happened even *after* the discussion group!"

Later that morning Olivia was prepared for surgery. Some of the other women had already been premedicated with a relaxant. Then orderlies took two women on stretchers from the room at a time. The minor surgery rooms were next to each other. The nurse gave Olivia an injection of morphine and scopolamine that made her very drowsy. She was transferred to a cart and wheeled toward a small operating room.

Olivia slipped over onto the operating table almost without noticing it. Everyone in the room wore surgical gowns, masks, and caps. The nurse scrubbed Olivia's chest and then draped her with many sterile green cloths. The cloth shield was placed between her neck and chest. Dr. Emick talked with her as he scrubbed his arms and hands at a basin near her head. Olivia had seen and spoken to him earlier in the morning and he had also talked to her husband.

Now, as Olivia watched him go over her chart, he almost seemed an old friend.

Recalling the experience later, she would say, "To my surprise, I was one of the first patients. I can remember drowsily smiling through the medications." Dr. Emick was gentle and humorous, and yet he projected an entirely professional feeling. He exuded confidence and said, "Now I want you to keep that smile for me. I'm going to make a small incision around your areola—the dark area around your nipple. It will be so fine no one will know that there has been a cut there to begin with."

"By the time I watched him put on his gown and gloves, I was really relaxed in spirit as well as by the medication. I trusted the man."

Olivia's head—behind the screen—was turned to one side, with her right arm bent underneath her head in order to give the surgeon as tight a breast area as possible to work on. Carefully, step by step, he explained the procedure. "There will be a slight prick of a needle and a small burning feeling as I inject the Xylocaine into your skin. Just relax. Okay, done. Now I'm going to make the incision. . . . You might feel a little pressure, but you shouldn't feel any pain. If you feel any pain at all, be sure to tell me, because I don't like heroines around this hospital!" Carefully, the surgeon made a half-moon incision around the bottom section of the areola after outlining it with a surgical pen. He spread the tissue with scissors and then used the electric cauterizer to stop the tissue from bleeding.

"I can remember smiling and talking with the nurse, who was holding my hand. I felt some pressure, and I asked Dr. Emick what he was doing. He said that he had inserted his finger into the incision to feel for the lump, that he had now located it and would remove it as quickly as he could. Looking back now, I was really struck by the humanness of this type of biopsy. Here I was the patient, relaxed, my anxiety obviously lessened. In talking to other women, I knew that I presented a marked contrast to those who had gone into a biopsy knowing that they would be put to sleep under a general anesthesia, but *not* knowing whether they would awaken from the event with or without a breast.

"The lump was removed, the wound cauterized to make the closure as clean and blood-free as possible, and then Dr. Emick said that he was taking time to make the sutures around the incision as fine as possible. I was then sprayed with something very cold which I was later to learn was an adhesive to help make the bandages stick to my skin. Before the pressure bandage was put in place, I asked to look at my breast. The nurse removed the cloth screen and I looked closely at the area around the areola. I could hardly tell the scalpel had been near the breast. Dr. Emick held up the lump in a jar to show me. He reminded me that the pathology report must be completed before any definitive answer could be given. I drowsily said 'Fine,' and thanked him for his concern.

"Clearly, the thorough and compassionate planning that had gone before had made the surgeon more aware of what he was doing. He had had personal contact with his patients; they were not just bodies covered with green sheets, wheeled unconscious into his domain, only a small part of their bodies exposed to him for identification . . . a breast. We were individual women. I was Olivia Newman, smiling drowsily at my surgeon and carrying on a conversation with him! He had established human contact; there had been a warm exchange and we were both humanly aware of each other. It was a very fortunate experience."

Olivia was taken back to her room to sleep off the medication that had been given her to relax her for the surgery while the biopsy was in progress. There had been a small discussion group between the husbands, focusing on what the biopsy had meant to their wives. They also learned that the possibility of cancer was utmost in the mind of any woman who was about to have a biopsy. The counselor spoke to the men about such things as how important a woman's breasts were to her. They meant femininity. They meant womanhood. They meant sex.

The counselor explained that psychologically many women consider their breasts as crucially important as men consider their penis and testicles. At first Clark was shocked by the analogy, but it was just that analogy which finally brought him full emotional understanding. How would the man feel, the counselor asked, if something suspicious had been discovered in his penis or testicles that suggested possible cancer, and the standard procedure in the medical profession was the immediate removal of one or both testicles and/or the penis? How would they all feel? Clark thought to himself, "My God, I have never considered just what an incredibly frightening experience this must be for Olivia." The counselor then discussed exactly what was happening to their wives in surgery. He also said he wanted the men to realize that their wives were very fortunate to be having only the biopsy. The psychological benefit of this method of minor surgery extended even further, he said. "Your wives do not have to arrange for several days of care for their families, as is necessary with the standard type of biopsy. There is little disruption of the family or professional life. In addition, the women will be going home with the feeling that they were not ill, which is a common feeling on the part of the patients who have to stay in the hospital for an average of 2.4 days for a standard type of biopsy."

The early discharge encouraged the women to feel well and therefore their convalescence was shorter. Another important fact was that cancerphobia—a fear of having cancer—was minimized by the two-step biopsy. He stressed that for a woman to sign a piece of paper saying, in effect, that she might wake up without a breast was terrifying even for the bravest. A traumatic experience like that could generate serious psychological upsets, even if a lump ultimately proved benign.

He also explained the team approach. And he made very clear to the husbands what their wives were going through, emphasizing that the women would often not be able to talk about it themselves because their emotions were so tangled. He emphasized that understanding and love on the part of the husbands help their wives not only after the biopsy procedure, but also during the few days' delay between biopsy, diagnosis, and any procedure to follow. Those few days would give the husbands time to understand, and to take part in helping their wives have more control over their own destiny. The counselor also said that, traditionally, men were supposed to be stronger and unemotional. But in a situation such as this, should they have any difficulties, they should feel free to call him night or day if there were any noticeable depression, distortion of their wives' personalities, problems with the children, or if they themselves had any problems.

The question naturally came up in the men's discussion group that not only was the *biopsy a serious trauma for husbands and wives, but there were the children to consider*. What were the husbands going to tell the children about their mothers being in the hospital . . . and coming home sleepy with bandages on their chests? The counselor explained that children were far wiser than adults gave them credit for. They might overhear a conversation on the telephone or, worse yet, hear from other children about what happened to their mothers. He said it was up to the parents, but that in his experience he'd found it was best to tell them the truth. There was certainly no need to go into elaborate details . . . just let them know what was going on. In that way, there would be no chance of the children misinterpreting anything.

In the event, he explained, that there was a cancer diagnosis, he felt that the facts of "Mommy's condition" should be explained simply to each child separately. Taking each one and telling him or her that Mommy was sick and why she was sick should be done in the simplest of terms. Each child, he continued, is a unique personality and would respond differently. Once the simple fact was stated, the child might or might not persist in questioning, One might just say, "Okay," and that would be that, while a brother or sister might well want to know more. In that case, the best way would be to answer the question, again as simply as possible—no more and no less. That way, the counselor went on, the children would not be excluded from the family by brooding on frightening thoughts about what was "happening to Mommy." Clark thought about what was said, and recalled his own childhood when his father had been seriously ill. Clark remembered he had felt totally left out and confused. In fact, he could vividly evoke his mother's hushed telephone conversations with neighbors concerning his father's illness, and he had never understood. When he had asked his mother, the answer had always been, "Daddy's sick." But he really didn't know why. When his father was in the hospital for a long time, Clark remembered that he had felt abandoned and afraid. He made a mental note to talk with the children and, if Olivia did have cancer, it would mean a long, hard pull for the entire family—not just for Olivia,

Clark Newman and the other husbands were not like the thousands of others who had never known anything about their wives' biopsies in terms of what it meant to them and the family.

Because of their discussion with the counselor, the husbands were not left outside in the waiting rooms of doctors' offices, or in the waiting rooms outside surgical doors, or in the "waiting rooms" of their homes. Instead, they were helped to understand that there were constructive things they could do for their wives besides just wait and hope. Regardless of the outcome of the day's biopsy, they were better prepared to help deal with whatever the results would bring.

A Personal Choice

When Clark Newman left the hospital with his still-drowsy wife on that Friday afternoon, he had come to know a great deal more about her, both physically and emotionally, than he had that morning. Although he was aware of the possibility that Olivia might have cancer, he felt they would both deal with that problem when and if it arose. At the moment, though, looking over at his wife of seventeen years, he experienced for the first time the privilege of being allowed to share a medical problem with her.

Olivia's appointment with the surgeon the following Monday was to check her wound and to receive the pathology report. Over the weekend, both Olivia and Clark decided to adhere to the surgeon's suggestion of taking things one step at a time—of not anticipating problems yet to be determined. However, on Sunday night when he and Olivia were in bed, she suddenly revealed the full range of her anxieties.

"What if it *is* breast cancer, Clark? I'm afraid to lose my breast, I'm afraid of not being able to handle it. . . . And what about us? And cancer? And the children?"

She could not hold back the tears. They talked but resolved nothing. Still, they *had* talked.

The receptionist greeted them both warmly and Olivia was directed to the examining room. Clark went with her. Olivia went through the now familiar routine of undressing and putting on the paper gown. She sat on the edge of the examining table, Clark by her side. The surgeon knocked and entered. As he washed his hands, he chatted pleasantly to Clark about racing cars, easing the obvious tension in the room.

It seemed amazing how far the considerate and gentle attitude of Dr. Emick had already extended minimized the anxiety of both his patient and her husband. He and the hospital team had let them both know as much as possible about what had taken place thus far. He was practicing a philosophy he had learned the hard way, and in which he believed strongly. When he first became aware that rushing people in and out of his office often resulted in tense and unhappy patients, he found that a little extra time spent in communicating with them—supplying them with information and a little warmth and support—usually made for psychologically more secure and thus physically better patients. It was certainly not always possible to give his patients all the support he wanted to give, so therefore he had given the ancillary staff at the hospital a green light to include his patients in counseling, social work, and volunteer programs that could supplement his own efforts. Admission to the hospital for anything, he understood, is a frightening ordeal. The team approach had an additional benefit, for Emick's teams also gave him feedback about his patients that he would not normally have had. It was a sort of reciprocal trade agreement—and satisfactory for both sides, yet he knew his "total approach" was somewhat atypical.

The surgeon who began to take the dressings from Olivia's breast knew what the word "cancer" would mean to Olivia and her family. To him, Olivia Newman was not an isolated problem —a diseased breast that needed treatment. She was a person who happened to have a diseased breast that needed to be treated, and who needed to be treated within the limits of her emotional and physical makeup. They had participated in an open relationship so far, but Olivia and Dr. Emick had become closer partners from the moment that the diagnosis of "infiltrating ductal carcinoma" had been made by the pathologist, as both he and the surgeon had examined Olivia's stained slide under the two-headed microscope, and Emick was about to make the nature of that new partnership clear.

As he gently removed the adhesive tape that held the pressure bandage to Olivia's chest, Dr. Emick spoke about his biopsy approach to Olivia's tumor.

"You know, it has been the tradition for a century to biopsy any breast tumor or lump through an incision directly overlying the clinically palpable lump. The time spent to identify and surgically remove such a mass was often found to be remarkably long. In some instances, the blood loss was more than desired, and in many of the cases the resulting scar brought permanent disfigurement for the patient. In the majority of cases, as I've already told you, general anesthesia with all its inherent complications was given for such a procedure."

It was not necessary to tell Olivia this, but it was in keeping with his gentleness and his consideration.

As the surgeon spoke, he deftly removed the bandage. "Good," he said, "there's no evidence of infection. It's healing well." Aside from a small bruise, the biopsy had left a fine incision line around the areola which, if no further surgical treatment were necessary, would fade into the areola's darker pigmentation. He removed the stitches. There were no problems.

Dr. Emick asked Olivia to dress and join him with her husband in his office. He paused reflectively, placed her chart on the desk, and looked her squarely in the eyes.

"I have your report. There is never an easy way to say this

. . . to tell you both. Your biopsy has proved the existence of a small cancerous tumor, less than one-half centimeter in size."

He stopped speaking. He knew Olivia and Clark would need some time.

Olivia dropped her head, shut her eyes. She thought, "Oh, my God, *no.*" Her stomach felt as though someone had hit her very hard. Her mind drifted off, from the room. . . . *"Cancer . . . what to do? Cancer . . . oh, my God no. It can't be."* Despite all her previous preparation, Olivia was stunned. Shocked. Numb.

Clark's reaction was instantaneous. He moved toward her and cradled her head in his arms. "Oh, my darling Olivia!"

Olivia took a deep breath, and her eyes met her surgeon's. There was a long moment's silence and then the doctor spoke.

"I'm very sorry, Olivia. Fortunately, it's a very small cancer. I know you need time to think about what to do. I've already spoken with your family physician. I don't think it's wise to present you both with all the possible procedures right here, right now. Many of them I know you're aware of already. There are some things, however, that I do want you to know.

"First of all, as I said, this is a very small cancer. The prognosis is most favorable for you because of its very early detection. You have time to go home, to discuss the matter between you. We also have time before we need to begin any definitive treatment. The medical literature shows no apparent evidence of any significant risks regarding survival as a result of this delay. Originally it was thought the time factor was critical, but we know better now. One of the main reasons we have time to talk and think about your treatment is because we will need to do what is known as a *metastatic examination* on you. That simply means we need to check for any widespread cancer elsewhere in your body.

"There are several things we'll need to do. We'll need some new tests to be completed, such as chest X-rays, as well as different types of blood tests. We will need to perform what is known as a bone scan. This is a very simple procedure that entails the

121

introduction of a weakly radioactive material into the bloodstream. The radioactive material is a compound that is concentrated by bones in areas where they are metabolically active. The radioactive material soon decays and becomes nonradioactive, so that there is only a minimal radiation exposure to the patient. You will lie on a table under a large machine. It moves slowly over the body . . . scanning . . . it is not in contact with your body. The machine detects radiations that are given off by the radioactive material. If the radioactive material is concentrated in an area of increased metabolic activity, this area will show up as a 'hot spot' on the bone scan. A film record is made of the relative intensities of radiation that are picked up by the scanner.

"Hot spots on a bone scan, of course, do not always mean cancer in the bones. Hot spots can be caused by many things besides cancer, including rather minor injuries. It takes special trained skill to interpert these scans properly. We will also perform a liver scan, for the same reason. Liver function tests will be included in your blood tests. These tests will also serve as something we call baseline studies. Like your original xerogram, the baseline studies mean that in the future we'll always be able to test you and compare the results with the past studies. The results of these X-rays, scans, and blood tests will, of course, have a direct influence on your form of treatment should you prove to have cancer elsewhere in your body. Do you feel there's anything you want to ask me?"

Olivia took another deep breath. "No, no, I don't think so. Not right now . . . I think we need to go home. I just think we need to go home and talk about this. I can't think about anything right now . . . I don't even know what to say."

The surgeon told her again of his sorrow and then he emphasized the need for the metastatic workup, telling her he would like to start these studies within the next two days.

Clark and Olivia stood up together. The surgeon rose, walked the two to the door, and put an arm around Olivia. "I want to remind you, Olivia, that your prognosis looks very good; it was a very small cancer. My receptionist will call you to arrange the testing schedule."

Olivia turned her head and just looked at him. It was left to Clark to thank Dr. Emick and say good-bye.

Nothing was said between Clark and Oliva in the car on the drive home. When they finally were able to talk, it was after a long embrace. Olivia spoke first—a flat and soft voice.

"Well, this is what it's all been about, isn't it?"

"Yes," said Clark. "I guess this is the day we've been preparing ourselves for."

In the ensuing days, they were able to talk over their feelings openly and warmly. Olivia completed the necessary and very thorough metastatic examination for disease elsewhere in her body. All the results were happily negative. With the help of their family doctor, Olivia chose to have a modified radical mastectomy with reconstruction of her breast at the time of surgery.

She was fortunate. Her surgeon and a plastic surgeon, thoroughly familiar with breast reconstruction, planned ahead before the time of her surgery. She had been well informed of the various forms of surgery available to her. The breast implant (an internal prosthesis) was a medical-grade silicone and rubber bag. After it was inserted under the skin, it was inflated with sterile salt water to match the size of the remaining breast. Thus, Olivia's right breast was reconstructed at the time of her cancer surgery. Her plastic surgeon also offered to attempt partial reconstruction of the nipple with tissue taken from the vaginal region sometime in the future, after healing was complete.

She was well aware that the reconstructive-surgery aspect of her choice was a departure from the norm. Most surgeons do not usually make any suggestions or plans for breast reconstruction— and if they do, it often means a delay of anywhere from six months to several years. Of course, Olivia's reconstructed breast would not look as good as the breast prior to mastectomy. It is unfortunate that some articles in the popular press have indicated that a perfect-looking breast can be expected. At this time, however, this remains unlikely. If the patient has more modest expectations, though, such as a simple restoration of the general contour of her breast, and more normal body symmetry, she is less likely to be disappointed with reconstruction.

Olivia's surgeons were aware that *planning is critical before surgery.* If the incisions are placed incorrectly by the general surgeon, the task of reconstructing the breast later will be difficult or impossible for the plastic surgeon.

One very important but little realized problem with breast reconstruction after cancer surgery, especially immediate reconstruction, is its legal aspect. The problem is this: A certain number of patients who undergo radical mastectomy, or any surgery for breast cancer, will experience recurrence of the cancer on the chest-wall site. These recurrences can be treated by radiation therapy or other modalities. However, it might prove to be more difficult to treat after reconstruction has been performed, and the patient should be informed of this. Since reconstruction is at present not generally in use, many doctors consider it beyond the realm of the "community standard of medical practice." Other doctors, taking the opposite view, would feel it is in fact above this standard.

Given this information, let us now consider a hypothetical case: A woman undergoes a modified radical mastectomy and then has her breast reconstructed. Months later a recurrence is found in the operated area. This would have occurred whether or not the reconstruction had taken place. The woman, however, does not understand this and becomes angry with her doctor. In this era of fee-hungry medical malpractice lawyers (who often keep up to 50 percent or even more of any settlement as their share of the take) a lawyer could step in and sue the surgeon for malpractice. Malpractice could be claimed, since the surgeon had performed an operation that did not conform to the community standard of medical practice. The lawyer might win, since breast reconstruction is currently controversial. There are some doctors who oppose it and might testify against the surgeon performing it.

Thus, the doctor's nightmare of medical malpractice suits is often translated into an impediment to better patient care. Many doctors may not want to undertake breast reconstruction after cancer surgery because of this medico-legal problem, all technical factors aside. Also, in all fairness, there is no long-term data available on women who have had this type of breast reconstruction. Medicine is still an art, not an exact science. Often it is impossible for the doctor to be in control of all the things that can possibly go wrong when he attempts to deliver good care to his patients. As you can see, Olivia's doctors were taking a risk for themselves when they rebuilt her breast. They were willing to do this in part because of an important factor in their relationship with Olivia—*mutual trust.* Just as Olivia trusted their judgment, they trusted hers in that they felt she would not sue them if she should have the misfortune to have a recurrence in the reconstructed area. They also informed Olivia of as many risks and unknowns as possible.

Olivia realized that the less-radical surgery offered her many advantages. Since the modified radial did not remove her pectoral muscles, there would be little, if any, deformity near the folds of her armpit, or axilla. The option of when the implants should be placed after the surgery was carefully explained to her. She could wait the six months to a year or more, or she could have the implant at the time of the actual cancer surgery. She asked Dr. Emick directly if there was any clear danger of having the implants inserted at the time of the surgery. He explained that the medical literature at this time gave many varied answers. No one knew unequivocally which was the most correct method.

After considerable discussion, Olivia decided that since there was no clear evidence against the practice of breast reconstruction immediately following surgery, she would "ride with the odds." In her mind, she felt this was acceptable—and it was a method she could handle emotionally. The realization that she had cancer was trauma enough. She would allow for the modified radical mastectomy since it included invesigation into the axillary nodes—which proved to be negative—but the thought of being left without a breast, she felt was too much.

Olivia was also aware that because her tumor was small, some surgeons suggested smaller surgeries such as a partial mastectomy. However, *this was her operation and her decision about her body.*

The plastic surgeon spent a great deal of time with Olivia so that she would fully understand the limitations of the procedure. He did this so that her expectations of the reconstructed breast with its inflated soft silicone and rubber implant would not exceed reality. The breast would not look as it had before the operation, but hopefully the cosmetic result would be acceptable.

By her own efforts, and with the help of her doctors, Olivia Newman had been fully informed. She knew the different forms and combinations of treatment available to her. She knew the pros and cons of each one. She had made an informed decision. No one had made the choice for her, as the choice was made for thousands of other women—such as Meg Land. Olivia made a choice within the limits of what she felt she could support, and her surgeon and family physician backed her. The breast surgeon and the plastic surgeon took care not to infringe on each other's roles, but they worked together to plan the best therapy and as fine a result for Olivia as possible.

She also received all the advantages of the hospital team-approach. Later, after she came home from the hospital, she received assistance from the Reach to Recovery program.

Olivia knew the possibility of recurrence, or even of widespread disease, faced her in the future. No matter what roads lay ahead, though, she would take the time to marshal the available information and evaluate the pros and cons of any future decisions, just as she had at this first crucial time.

Her doctors had made it clear to both Olivia and Clark that biannual examinations, consisting of chest X-rays, scans, blood tests, etc., would be necessary for the rest of her life. She would have to live with the thought of the possible recurrence of cancer. She was prepared by her doctors to examine herself even more closely than before the diagnosis. Olivia was now in the highest-risk group of all. Between visits to her doctors for examinations, she would have to be her own doctor, assuming responsibility for her body, looking for any changes at all—any new lumps, soreness, bone pain, weight loss, and the dozen of other signs her doctor had written down for her. Her husband would need to take an active interest, too, always on the lookout for personality changes, alteration of mood, or depression. It would be a joint effort.

Facing the Future—Other Choices

Since Olivia's cancer had been diagnosed early, she might well have been a candidate for a combination of partial mastectomy with radiation therapy and/or chemotherapy. If her choice had been radiation therapy, her surgeons, the radiation therapist, and the family physician would have planned her treatment together. She would not have been an abandoned patient being shuffled off to one specialist or another. She would have been brought in on some of the finer details of radiation therapy. She would have discovered that the techniques of radiation therapy vary considerably at different hospitals and in different cases, but more importantly she would have become aware that radiation therapy is a local method of treatment only. That is to say, it only affects a cancer contained within the irradiated area.

Olivia would have been told that radiation therapy can be used to treat breast cancer as a primary method of attempting to curb the disease. This is often done when the patient refuses surgery, is inoperable because of poor general health, or has inflammatory carcinoma, the rare variant of breast cancer discussed in the Appendix. The results of this treatment vary greatly from case to case.

She would have learned that a breast that has been given enough radiation to kill a tumor will generally not look or feel like a normal breast. The overlying skin will probably be atrophic, hyperpigmented (darker), and perhaps covered with tiny new blood vessels. The breast itself might be firm and perhaps deformed, depending on the original site and size of the tumor.

As a primary mode of therapy, irradiation alone is often considered suboptimum treatment. Nonetheless, Olivia would have been cautioned that this skeptical attitude is not shared by some radiotherapists. Thus, the entire field of radiation therapy in the treatment of breast cancer is also in controversy.

Olivia would have been aware of the second way radiation is used—as a supplement to surgery. Irradiation can be used prior to surgery to shrink a very large, long-neglected tumor so that it becomes technically feasible for the surgeon to remove it. Or it can also be used after surgery if the doctor thinks there is a danger of a recurrence at the scar site, residual disease in the axilla, disease in the internal mammary chain of nodes, or disease in the lymph nodes above the clavicle.

Olivia might also discover that a third way radiation can be used is as a palliative method of therapy. For example, a woman with advanced, incurable disease can often be greatly assisted by judicious use of irradiation. A common situation is that of a woman who has breast cancer which has spread to the bones and is eroding them, causing pain and the possibility of a fracture. Irradiation will usually relieve the pain and may prevent the development of an incapacitating fracture. The fracture again develops because of erosion to the bones—which leads to weakness or brittleness. The radiation is somehow able to slow the erosion and strengthen the bones.

Irradiation would have made it much more difficult for the plastic surgeon to reconstruct Olivia's breast. *The decision as to*

*whether a given patient should have radiation therapy combined
with surgery should be made by her surgeon, radiation therapist,
and family doctor as they work together with the woman to plan
her total treatment.*

Olivia Newman had heard of *chemotherapy* and had been informed about it in a general way by her family doctor and her
surgeon. She learned that chemotherapy was usually used as a
method of treating patients with advanced, widespread disease.
Some chemotherapy agents appeared to have an effect on the term
of survival, others provide some remissions, still others sometimes
seemed to cure, but the majority had little effect on long-term
survival rates. None of the drugs available at this time are without
adverse effects on body tissues. These toxic qualities often limit
use. However, progress is being made with dozens of well-con-
trolled studies being carried out around the world.

Chemotherapy in breast cancer treatment has traditionally been
used when widespread cancer elsewhere in the body was noted.
However, Olivia learned that *many doctors are now using drug
therapy as soon as breast cancer is diagnosed.* Evidence mounts
that seems to indicate that micrometastases, cancers so small that
they cannot be detected, may be present in the body when the
breast cancer diagnosis is first made. This theory has prompted
doctors to start chemotherapy at once.

The idea behind the use of chemotherapy is to lower the cancer-
cell multiplication or to destroy the cancer cells themselves. Since
no two patients are the same, each will respond differently to these
drugs. The goal in chemotherapy treatment is to prolong survival
and hope for remission and possibly cure. Olivia was well aware
that chemotherapy should not be undertaken lightly, since it is
usually a difficult treatment. Even with the mildest forms of
therapy there may be considerable side effects. Depending on the
drug and the dosage, chemotherapy can cause nausea, fatigue,
hair loss, damage to the heart, bladder, and other organs, bone
marrow depression and lowered blood cell count. The chemicals
used are undeniable toxic, and in doing their job of attacking

cancer cells, they may well damage healthy tissue as well. Recently there has been much sensational exposure of the results of chemotherapy studies in Italy and the United States. The reports are encouraging, but the research is too new to give the long-term answers that are essential. As of today there is no "magic cure" for breast cancer, but chemotherapy certainly offers one of the most promising hopes.

Olivia had known chemotherapy entailed the administration of drugs. Now she learned how potent these drugs were and that they often had serious side effects. It was because of the possible side effects that patients had to be monitored very carefully while the drugs were being administered. There was even a specialist who presided over the patient during such treatment. He was known as a "medical oncologist." Olivia's family doctor told her he had not had sufficient training in the area of medicine, and, therefore, *if she ever needed chemotherapy it would have to be with the guidance of an oncologist.* She learned that the administration of hormone therapy for cancer also fell under the expertise of an oncologist. Olivia was advised that medical oncology is a new field of medicine. There are few board certified oncologists in the United States at this time. Her doctor told her that if she should move to a community that did not have an oncologist, she should seek a consultation with one from a cancer center, medical school, or large medical center. The main reason behind her doctor's word of caution made sense. Chemotherapy is usually a highly toxic form of cancer treatment, and the patient must be constantly medically monitored. It is also an ever-changing field. New forms of therapy may not always reach the doctors in areas away from a big center for many months. Also, doctors not familiar with chemotherapy advances in cancer therapy may inadvertently withhold up-to-date treatment from a patient.

It became clear to Olivia that there were many, many forms and combinations of treatments. She also knew that there was *no guarantee she would be free of cancer in her lifetime.* She might have to face repeated decisions regarding different forms of treatment should she have a recurrence of the disease or should it spread throughout her body. There was an endless controversy about all of the treatments. Many doctors initiated chemotherapy at the onset of breast cancer. Some waited until there was further evidence of disease in the body. Some physicians advocated using immunotherapy, an experimental form of treatment that was meant to help the patient's body reject its own cancer. Immunotherapy simply was an assistant method to encourage the body's own natural immunity against disease. Yet, some doctors advised against it. Cancer and its treatment made up a strange and baffling world. Olivia found that it took a great deal of strength not only to deal with the fact that she was now a cancer patient, but also to begin to understand that there were many varied forms of treatment—and no guarantees with any of them. She valued immensely the philosophy that had been imparted to her by her doctor: "One step at a time."

Olivia's husband not only had a chance to participate in his wife's decision and share her dilemma, he also had the opportunity to speak several times to a cancer psychologist. He was able to understand some of the emotional responses he could expect from his wife, how best to inform the children, and how to try to keep the dialogue open with Olivia. He fully understood that his wife might react in a constantly changing pattern. He was prepared for such mood shifts as depression, anger, denial, and perhaps even irrational behavior. Clark discovered that the psychological aspects of breast cancer are as unpredictable as the disease, but, unlike many husbands, he was prepared for the worst or the best. He would understand that his initial encounter with cancer, and with emotionally upsetting and draining decision-making might well continue. Since there are no laws concerning cancer, and since it is always unknown who will survive and who will not, it is possible Olivia would face more decisions that would affect her destiny. Having shared so directly in the first stage of her struggle, he knew these decisions would not just involve Olivia; they would involve him, too.

Jane Cowles

One Cancer Patient's View

Shortly after Olivia's surgery she received a letter from a friend. In it was a statement from a cancer patient about her own experience. To Olivia's mind this patient's choice had been her own, and Olivia could easily understand it. She read the letter aloud to Clark:

The question has been put to me by acquaintances as well as by members of the medical profession—in short, "Why didn't you have a mastectomy?"

Obviously there cannot be a concise and totally rational response. A brief medical history must precede any thorough explanation. In my specific case, a "benign lump" was removed in January, 1973.

After thoroughly researching the facts—both obvious ones and the papers, articles, and monographs of specialists and doctors—information not readily available to the public—I came to the conclusion that there definitely was an underground battle raging among doctors in the field of cancer treatment. It appeared that there were far too many unanswered questions. Why did one cancer patient doomed to a few short years by the doctors survive, while another, whose prognosis looked favorable, quickly succumb to the dread disease? Both had been similarly treated. It appeared to me that doctors had no difficulty diagnosing the presence of cancer, treating it with many modalities such as surgery, radiation, and chemotherapy. However, there is where the point of departure came. There were just too many variables in breast cancer therapy. Good reasons could be found for all of the treatments—or for little treatment at all.

After my first biopsy, I continued to pursue my quest for valid facts and enlightenment. I began to make a case for myself. Slowly it took shape. Personally, I doubted whether I could ever accept amputation as an attempt to arrest my cancer, even if I should become a "cancer statistic" in the future. I realized that in many cases, aggressive surgical methods did not necessarily seem to be bringing about any remarkable success. Since the medical profession approached cancer from a statistical standpoint, the doctors were and still are treating it on a purely "nonindividualistic" basis. In other words, the formula is: Malignant lump equals mastectomy. I felt being treated as a statistic was detrimental physically as well as psychologically.

June of 1973 brought the onset of summer and the agony of decision. My newfound convictions were put to the test. An examination with mammograms indicated a suspicious lesion in the same breast from which the benign lump had been removed. Once again, a biopsy would be necessary. The pressure was mounting. My physician felt that if, in fact, the lump were to be malignant, a mastectomy was the method of treatment most favored. I couldn't imagine myself accepting amputation in the future. I doubted in the long run that it would do much good.

The lump was small, but it was malignant. After the biopsy, I finally summoned enough strength to convince the doctors that I truly did not want and would not give my approval for a mastectomy to be performed. With this realization, they suggested an alternative—radiation therapy.

The radiation therapy was a valid form of treatment. I was confident it was highly likely that I would be facing similar decisions sometime in the future. It is a fact that cancer recurs with or without a mastectomy in a large majority of cases. I knew that psychologically I had to be healthy in order to meet the physical challenges cancer would or could bring about. A mastectomy and its resulting damage did not—for me—encourage a sense of well-being and wholeness of spirit. The choice was radiation therapy or a mastectomy. I chose radiation therapy.

Radiation treatments commenced. I tolerated it well, and by

the end of the summer I realized that not the radiation but coping with the idea that I had cancer was far more tedious and debilitating. It would be exactly eighteen months before I really felt the full impact and effect of precisely how destructive this disease could be to my mental outlook.

The doctors watched me closely with follow-up examinations and X rays, and there were many consultations. The doctors were not in agreement as to whether a favorable prognosis was indicated. They adopted a wait and see attitude.

Several months after the radiation therapy had been completed, I had some specific complaints. My ribs ached and I was uncomfortable. Only then did I know how difficult it would be for me to get a commitment as to exactly what my status was physically.

Actually, the reason for the specialists' vacillation was well founded. They simply didn't know. My original premise—that there was a plethora of opinions on the treatment of cancer—was a reality! It wasn't that anyone was right or wrong, they just couldn't be sure. Some advocated another biopsy of the ribs; others said no. I decided to stick with no biopsy. The chances were, if cancer was still in the chest wall, other symptoms would very probably show up soon anyway.

In 1974, 18 months after the primary lesion was diagnosed as malignant, my chest cavity filled with fluid. This is commonly known in medical circles as a "pleural effusion." After hospitalization, the fluid was removed and biopsied. The fluid proved to be malignant. Once again, the disagreement among the specialists began. Some advocated hormonal therapy, others an aggressive form of chemotherapy. I knew aggressive chemotherapy would be arduous and would sap my strength; however, I felt no harm could be done by trying it because I always had the option of discontinuing.

Presently, I am taking chemotherapy. It is everything I expected and more. It has taken its toll, but it's working. There is no doubt that it would be foolish and impossible for anyone, including the doctors, to say that a mastectomy would have saved me from further treatment or the recurrence of cancer. Since it recurred so rapidly, it seems that cancer was present in my body at the time of the original diagnosis, and no matter how radical the surgery might have been, it certainly could not have totally arrested the disease. I can only be sustained by what my intuition told me originally. I'm thankful that I didn't have to struggle with the rehabilitative processes that follow a mastectomy in addition to all the other discomforts physically and mentally that I have experienced.

I know there are other women who have decided against a mastectomy. I am sure they began uninformed and, by persevering, arrived at some startling facts. They know that these facts are not easily obtained. The majority of women, when faced with a malignancy, gratefully accept surgery. Some live to regret their decision and many more are content that they did the right thing. Out of all these women, no one knows how many were really informed and presented with both sides of the issue. For that is all a woman should really have. *She can never be fully assured that by choosing one treatment over another she will be cured.* Psychologically, she will always carry the burden that at any time she may face the disease again. It is sad that counseling is available for mastectomy patients *after* surgery and not before. The emphasis is on the prosthesis—regaining use of the arm again. It is sad that many doctors brush off the mental and emotional complications that most cancer patients experience. One sees the attitude in some doctors that the patient should be thankful she is alive, no matter what the physical or mental cost. *The quality of the way one lives a life is pushed aside for the prevailing philosophy that all that matters is survival:* "No matter what condition you may be in, you are still a member of the human race." No one would deny that the mental outlook of a cancer patient plays a major role in her physical progress. However, the patient is often expected to draw on her own resources with no external assistance. Physicians will say they are too busy handling the disease itself.

The point to be made in answering the question "Why didn't I opt for radical surgery?" is that *I am not suggesting that anyone should be convinced to follow my route,* only that they should be as *fully informed as humanly possible.* Too often, because of the nature of the disease, women are left in the dark while physicians are rushing to arrest the cancer. The truth is that rapid advances are being made in the field of cancer treatment. Because of these advances, the methods available are continually being updated. Every woman has the right to the treatment she feels is *best for her, and only she can decide what that is.* However, one cannot arrive at a proper decision if she is denied the full story. Many doctors say they don't wish to tell all because it only confuses the patient. A doctor should not be allowed to take that stand. Realistically, a doctor in this era of sophisticated medicine must treat the whole patient. A doctor is not only being reimbursed for a specific skill, but for a total composite of knowledge gained through years of study and experience. This must be passed on to the patient. Otherwise, the patient has experienced assembly-line medicine.

It is also necessary to suggest that my life-style did not influence my decision not to have a mastectomy. I am married, in my early 30's, and a mother. I believe that had I been in my late 50's and approaching the autumn of my life, I still would have made essentially the same decision.

I don't want to give the impression that an indictment should be made solely against the medical profession; for the most part, many doctors are not really aware that they are withholding pertinent information from their women patients. Telling a bare minimum has become a conditional reflex. When valid medical facts are withheld, one always runs the danger of picking up many fallacies passed along from friend to friend. However, the time has come for the facts to be bared, no matter how brutal they sound. There must be a renewal of respect for the total person. Once we stop thinking in terms of organs, limbs, etc., we will be on a more humane wavelength. The numbers of women who entirely avoid medical assistance out of fear of a mastectomy is shocking! The National Cancer Institute as well as the American Medical Association would like to believe that they are reaching all women regarding cancer detection in the breast. The truth is, they are not reaching enough. Perhaps it's time to ask why.

THREE

The Responsibility Is Yours

We have looked into the lives of two women—Meg Land and Olivia Newman—at a time of crisis for each of them. It is obvious that although both women were exposed to the sophisticated attitudes of today's medicine, Olivia Newman definitely participated in the outcome of her particular situation. She was not alone, however. Olivia received the full benefit of concerned doctors who held her total best interest at heart, not their own. The purpose of presenting the cases of Meg Land and Olivia Newman was not to take sides in a medical dispute, but to point out that women should have access to medical information when they are asked to be involved in medical decisions.

Usually most of the informational conversations occur in the doctor's office. It is at this time that the woman should not be subjected to any undue pressure or duress concerning any possible surgical procedures. This duress or even coercion can also come about because the doctor does not fully present all aspects of the different procedures, thereby seemingly dismissing different forms of treatment and pushing his preferred treatment upon the patient, so that in reality she really had not partaken in any form of consent at that time.

Since the procedure undergone by Mrs. Ford, women will probably have a difficult time discussing possible alternative treatments to breast cancer with their doctors. However, a woman should not let her physician lead her to a decision which is totally biased by the doctor's beliefs—it does not relieve him of his duty of disclosure to the patient.

I have tried to provide you with as much information as possible via several vehicles. Some of the information may have been confusing and possibly unpleasant. It involved you so that you could be the beneficiaries of knowledge too often kept within the confines of the medical community. Many times the difficulty in relaying important information to the laywoman is the fault of the system. It is sometimes years before medical information is obtained, written up first in medical journals with a limited circulation, then finally put into community practice.

This book has given you as much knowledge as possible on current medical information, medical controversies concerning the entire breast cancer experience and, in particular, about informed consent. In writing it, it has been my hope that you will be a more active participant in what happens to your body. I hope the book has raised questions in your mind, but more importantly, it has given you a head start on how you might go about staying in charge of your body. Unfortunately, many of you will run up against concrete walls with your own doctors. Don't give up. Doctors are slowly becoming attuned to the fact that their female patients usually want to know about the parameters of their treatment, know the side effects, and participate in decision-making policy, especially when it concerns the quality of their lives, and their destinies.

Sometimes doctors overlook the total person in concentrating on a particular medical problem. It is therefore essential that you express to your doctor how you feel about certain treatments, especially when the treatment may affect your emotional state, quality of life, or family structure. *You have the right to ask for as much information as possible when considering something as serious as biopsy or breast tumor removal*. This is an individual matter for you. Some of you may not want to know, may prefer to leave everything in your doctors' hands, but some of you indeed will want to know everything that is going on. Your frank, open communication to your doctor is a signal to him. He can't read your mind.

It is certainly not the fault of your doctor that breast cancer and breast cancer treatments are such enigmas. However, as the cancer patient states in the end of this book, if a patient really wants to know what is going on, her doctor should attempt to reveal the full story and not confuse her with double-talk and evasive answers.

As frightening as it may be for me to know what's actually going on, I personally would rather be informed in order to plan my life accordingly. I am, at a very young age, in a high-risk category. I have a family history of breast cancer, I am not married, I have no children, and because of a recent screening xerogram I must be monitored closely every six months. No one is going to watch out for me but me. No one can watch out for you but you.

You now have much of the information necessary. I plead with you to be responsible and do everything you can within your control to take proper care of yourself. I know it's sometimes a bore to examine your breasts on a monthly basis, but try to do so. At first you may think it is impossible to examine your breasts yourself, to know them well. But you'll get better and better at self-examination as you practice it. Like anything, once you get into a routine of doing something important, your mind will set an automatic clock. You'll remember fairly effortlessly that it is time to check your breasts. You may also, as I am now doing, have to converse with your doctor about commencing baseline xerogram studies in order to have them available to compare them over the ensuing years for any possible changes. Even though you might fall into the high-risk category, there is no reason to dwell on it—only to be aware of it and act accordingly. If, by breast self-examination and screen xerography, you can lessen the chance of advanced breast cancer, it would be foolish and irresponsible not to take an active interest in your future.

I know it takes courage to speak up to your doctor, and that it is sometimes a frightening experience. I myself have forgotten important questions I felt required answers and I, too, have been intimidated by doctors. It is indeed a helpless feeling when a domineering doctor makes a medical pronouncement and by his manner effectively closes the door while you sit in front of him. I finally decided that too many questions remained, to me, unanswered, and I didn't particularly enjoy the feeling that some of my doctors were rushing me out the door. Suddenly I felt shortchanged. So I now set up appointments seriously, by telling a receptionist that I wish to speak with the doctor after I see him. This allows her to schedule me a little extra time. If she asks, "What about?" I just say, "It's personal"—and it is.

In completing this book I began to think of ways that you could brace yourselves for encountering your doctor, if you were having a difficult time. Perhaps you could get together with a few women, or even form a women's group, and do a little role-playing on "how to speak with your doctor." If that's not your style, try runthroughs with your husband, a social worker, a psychologist, or a friend—or perhaps just alone with yourself in front of a mirror. If need be, take someone along with you. And if you are really worried and tend to blot things out from anxiety, take a tape recorder with you and ask the doctor to explain things in detail. These are only a few suggestions, and you can evolve any method that works best for you, *but get what you want from your doctor without strangling him for time—be reasonable.*

Remember, you cannot be legally forced to sign any consent form for any surgery. You do not have to have a biopsy done under a general anesthesia. If this, and problems of examinations from your doctor, are a problem, you can do the following things to find new doctors who will respect your wishes: Contact the chiefs of surgery in the hospitals or medical centers in your area, or medical schools, women's organizations, medical societies, etc. If your doctor is not responsive and will not actively inform you of all aspects of consent, then it may be necessary to obtain legal help.

Please remember that if you find a lump, *three out of four lumps are not cancerous.* Because you have that information, however, *does not mean you should wait.* See your doctor at once! The earlier you have a biopsy, the better off you are. Recall cancer's swift doubling time. One cancer cell times two is very small, but when a cluster of cells is big enough to detect, it can snowball into something very large.

Given the information in this book, try to realize that *you should not panic or let anyone else panic you.* This is more easily said, of course, when there is nothing wrong. But if you should find yourself in a situation in which you need a biopsy, and sometimes thermograms as well, xerograms should be made *before* the biopsy to add as much as possible to the clinical information your doctor has. This will also provide a picture of what your breast looks like before the biopsy. It will probably be a struggle, but if you are willing, and your surgeon agrees, attempt to have the biopsy using the local anesthetic method unless there is some very serious medical indication against it, or unless you absolutely do not want to be semiawake during the biopsy.

Remember, if you do have a positive biopsy, everyone is going to be in a gigantic hurry. You may well be frightened, and confused, too. So mark up this book, and consult the index and suggestions on page 151.

Plan ahead. Find a physician you can communicate with. It is your life, and it could mean a part of your body if you encounter cancer. You have the right, in this country, to expect the best treatment, but you must organize yourself and see that good treatment is available to you. Once you have prepared yourself, you will be much less afraid. You will have control over your destiny. You will be stronger and with this strength take better care of yourself.

Despite the information and ideas set forth in this book, the fact remains that the first and most immediate responsibility rests squarely on the shoulders of the woman herself. It is her breast, her health, her life, and her responsibility. Dr. William Glasser, noted West Coast psychiatrist and educator, offers the following comments written especially for this book:

In this book, women will be given some very firm advice—examine your breasts monthly and look for a lump, dimples, asymmetry, or any other abnormalities. Some will take this advice and it could be life-saving. Why won't all women? If women are reading these words then they must be interested, yet still after a few breast self-examinations, many will not continue. If a woman were sitting across from me here in my office and I asked her why, she could be evasive. She would say, I am right, or that she will start, but she still may not. Simply stating it, she is afraid—afraid she will find something and lose a breast. A woman is not then afraid she will lose her life—none of us who is healthy fears that—what she is afraid of is the disfigurement which may come, but, as this book shows, does not have to accompany the loss of a breast. . . . What is at the heart of a woman's refusal to examine her breasts regularly is that she does not want to see her own downfall. She doesn't want to take her fate into her own hands. Leave it to chance. Leave it to someone else. It's simply too much responsibility for her to handle.

My argument is this—who is more important to a woman than herself? In her mind maybe her children, possibly her husband are more important. Because they are, she examines them. She constantly looks out for *their* health—she does this because she loves them and she needs them. Well, they need her. They will watch over her but they can't examine her breast. Or, if a husband could, and would, a woman probably wouldn't want him to. That's not the way she wants her breasts handled by him—so I say, as she watches over them, and they watch over her because they need her—she must examine her own breasts because they can't do this for her. This much a woman has to do for herself—and if she is alone, the argument is even stronger—then, she must be the most important person to herself.

So each month women should say to themselves—they love me, they need me, but this they can't do for me—no one can do it but me. I love them and I need them, so I will do it for myself.

FOUR

Points You Should Remember

Points You Should Remember

Some Hints on How to Get
The System to Give You Better Care

1. Visit your doctor for a breast examination.
2. Ask him to set up regular breast examination schedules.
3. Ask him to show you the proper technique for breast self-examination. See figures 4–9, pages 75 to 83)
4. Practice monthly breast self-examination faithfully. Even if you have lumpy breasts, you will learn what is normal or abnormal. There is no excuse for not practicing self-examination.
5. If you fall into a high-risk category, ask your doctor about baseline screening mammography or xerography.
6. If you discover a lump, don't panic! See your doctor or breast specialist.
7. Don't be rushed by anyone. *Stay in control.*
8. If you should need a biopsy, insist that you have a mammogram or xerogram first (and ask about a thermogram as well). After the biopsy, the tissue that was removed will leave scar tissue inside the breast. Therefore, a xerogram is made before the biopsy so that any future changes in the xerogram can be compared to the originals.
9. It may be a difficult task but try to have your biopsy using the local anesthetic method unless otherwise indicated. A very deep

lump, psychological fears, or the desire to be alseep would be reasons to have a general anesthetic.

10. Always wait for the permanent pathology report. The results may indicate a change in treatment plans.

11. Attempt to include your husband or those close to you in any biopsy or treatment procedure discussions. Make certain you both understand everything that is about to take place.

12. Seek a consultation with a second physician or surgeon, one who does not have a financial involvement in the consultation. (A small fee can be agreed upon.)

13. It is essential not to have any breast cancer treatment without first obtaining a check for cancer elsewhere in the body— a check known as a metastatic workup. It can dramatically alter the choice of treatment.

14. The purpose of the metastatic workup is to check for widespread cancer and to provide a comparison study for evaluation in the future.

15. Don't let your doctor bully you—it's your body.

16. If you feel you can't handle your doctor, take your friend, husband, sister, etc., with you to his office.

17. Seek outside help from social workers, psychologists, your family doctor, or clergymen to assist you with any underlying difficulties. This is very important.

18. If you are confused, and living in a small community, consultation and information are only a phone call away. Call a major research center or hospital. Speak to someone who is an expert.

19. Know what is being done to your body before it is done.

20. If your doctor won't do the following things, perhaps you should entertain the thought of looking for a new one:
- examine your breast thoroughly
- show you how to examine your breasts
- arrange for xerograms if needed
- agree to biopsy first—treatment second
- wait for a permanent pathology report

- allow you to refuse to sign any papers saying that things go his way or no way at all
- do a metastatic workup before surgery
- spend time with you (but don't choke him with overtime—much of the responsibility there lies with you)
- consult with another doctor
- encourage you to seek other opinions (this means responsible opinions, not shopping for doctors)
- discuss your case, treatment, and diagnosis with you in depth.

21. Take an active part in the responsibility for your body. It's your body—it belongs to you—you can't expect other people to be as responsible as you should be.

22. Remember that medical attitudes are constantly changing. Make an effort to know as much as possible about new techniques and treatments. Take an active interest in your health.

FIVE

Appendices

1. The Breast Cancer Problem

Cancer of the breast is a major killer of women in the United States. It is the most common malignancy in females. The American Cancer Society states that 33,000 women died from it in 1975. Ninety thousand new cases will be reported this year and, with national awareness of the disease bringing more women into hospitals, clinics, and doctors' offices, the number of cases is steadily increasing. A woman in this country stands an overall 7 percent chance of having breast cancer in her lifetime. In other words, about one out of every fourteen women will be affected.

What is cancer? More specifically, what is breast cancer? Curious as it may seem, cancer is a disease concept very difficult to define. We can work with a preliminary definition that cancer is a disease process in which a group of cells in the body have altered from the normal cells in the following ways:

They grow and divide in an unrestrained fashion.

They are said to grow "autonomously"—that is, without regard for the needs of the rest of the body. One of the problems with cancer cells is that they are in business for themselves. They have no respect for the "organization."

Under the microscope, they look different from normal cells.

Often they are described as "bizarre." For example, they may be very much smaller or very much larger than the cells from which they come.

Along with the different appearance, the cells lose the ability to perform the functions for which they were originally intended. In leukemia, for example, although the body is literally overrun with abnormal white blood cells, these cells cannot protect the body against infection as normal white cells do. Indeed, the patient with leukemia often dies from infection.

As they grow, cancer cells have a tendency to invade and destroy other nearby organs.

They have a tendency to spread to other, often distant areas of the body. This phenomenon is known as metastasis.

For the moment, we are going to have to be content with this as perspective on the disease, but as we will discover, cancer is far more capricious and unpredictable than you might infer from this more or less simple explanation.

Interestingly and disturbingly, when the American Cancer Society correlated empirical studies of whole populations of women they identified classes of women who run a higher risk than normal of developing cancer of the breast and dying from it.

Higher-risk women include those who have one or more of the following characteristics: in upper socioeconomic groups, Jewish, unmarried, infertile, over the age of thirty-five, have one or two children, whose first pregnancy occurred after their twenty-fifth birthday, whose menarche (onset of menstrual periods) occurred before their twelfth birthday, who had been menstruating for thirty or more years, whose mothers or sisters had breast cancer. So if we wanted to take a typical example of a woman who might be particularly aware of the possibility of breast cancer, she would be a Jewish suburban housewife, over thirty-five, with two children, the first of whom was born when she was twenty-eight, who menstruated for the first time at the age of ten, whose menstrual periods continue, and whose sister and/or mother had breast cancer. No one understands why this should be. Equally, no one understands why women who represent the following are lower-risk women: married women, women with many children, women under thirty-five, those whose children were born before their twenty-fifth birthday, women whose menstrual periods began after their fifteenth birthday, women who continue to menstruate for more than thirty years, and women whose ovarian functions have been impaired or destroyed either by surgery or by radiation therapy.

No relationship between taking birth control pills and the risk of development of breast cancer has been found.

2. Breasts Are Fun to Know About

Before going much further, before examining what cancer of the breast is and how to deal with it, bear with a brief lesson in anatomy. *It is important for you to understand your own body.* Sadly and all too frequently, some of the things you must understand in order to make vital decisions about your destiny are simply not going to be told you by your doctor. Most frequently, he just doesn't have the time, often he doesn't feel it necessary; but the breast is a fascinating and dynamic organ.

The female breast is actually a modified sweat gland. It begins to develop in the human embryo as a small swelling known as the mammary ridge. There are two parallel mammary ridges found on the underside of the developing embryo as early as the sixth week of its life. Part of each mammary ridge enlarges and extends downward into the area beneath the skin of the embryo and then into the underlying connective tissue. This primordial downgrowth branches to produce approximately sixteen to twenty-four secondary sprouts. Fat cells are then deposited around these sprouts. Remember, at this moment in the growth of the embryo, the structure is microscopic. As the embryo grows, becomes a fetus, and is ultimately delivered as a baby, the microscopic breasts grow with it to a size that begins to be recognizable as a breast. At birth there is no obvious difference between a male and female breast.

The first profound change in the female breast takes place at puberty. Real development begins to take place under the influence of increased production of estrogens (female sex hormones) by the ovaries. The estrogens stimulate growth and branching of the duct system of the breast, growth of the supportive tissues of the breast, and deposits of fat to make the breasts larger. The estrogens also cause a slight darkening of the areola—the thicker skin around the nipple.

Several years after the beginning of menstruation, the woman's breast reaches an adult, or "resting," state. It has a fairly well developed duct system, but the actual cells that secrete milk are not yet present in any great quantity. Even though the breast is said to be "resting" during this time, it undergoes cyclic changes during the menstrual cycle, reinforcing the notion that the breast is a dynamic organ. With the profound hormonal stimulus of pregnancy, the duct system branches and rebranches. Also, the cells that will secrete milk are formed. They are arranged in clusters called alveoli, which empty into the milk ducts. The pregnant breasts enlarge and the nipples darken further.

After childbirth, the breast is capable of secreting milk. This postpartum breast is functionally different from the pregnant breast. Continued secretion of milk is dependent on continued emptying of the breast, usually by suckling by the infant. This postpartum, or lactating, breast regresses partially after cessation of breast feeding. With age, the breast gland shrinks and the skin loses its elasticity. The menopause accelerates this atrophy, probably due to the deficiency of estrogens and progesterone—another female hormone.

So now, understanding how the breast develops and changes through the life cycle, it is worthwhile to examine the anatomy of the adult female breast. This is critical, for it forms the backdrop of the stage setting on which the drama of disease will be played.

The breast, which we celebrate as the female chest's most dramatic and admired feature, is not really round; it is roughly conical. Sitting at the top of the cone is the nipple, and surrounding the nipple is a dark pigmented circle of slightly thicker skin known as the areola. The breast is not geometrical. It is rounded and it has an extension that tapers off toward the armpit. This extension, or "tail," is called the "axillary tail," since in medical jargon the armpit is called the axilla. As a random but interesting note, a woman's left breast is often larger than the right one. No one knows why.

For someone not a doctor to look inside the breast is a formidable task, but important and worthwhile. Bring along your imagination. First, here is a short list of the major elements of the female breast and the briefest of explanations of why each is essential to understand.

Fat and connective tissue provide both the bulk of the resting adult breast and some of its support. Being soft and pliable, they allow it some freedom of movement. If you were to see breast fat, it would look familiar: It is like fat on a steak. For its part, the connective tissue resembles the thin "strippy" gristle apparent in less elegant slices of meat at the butcher's counter.

Alveoli are clusters of milk-producing cells. They empty into the ducts of the breast, which carry the milk to the nipple. The cells that line the ducts are most often the site of origin of breast cancer.

Arteries bring fresh blood to the breast and the *veins* carry it away.

The *lymphatic drainage* system of the breast consists of a network of tiny tubes, usually much thinner than the very finest human hair. They carry certain white blood cells and a clear fluid called lymph away from the breast. Because they can also carry cancer cells away from the breast to other parts of the body, we will come back to the lymphatic system for a more concentrated discussion.

Now let's imagine that the skin over the breast is gone. (See figure 13, page 164) What is visible is mostly fat and connective

Figure 13

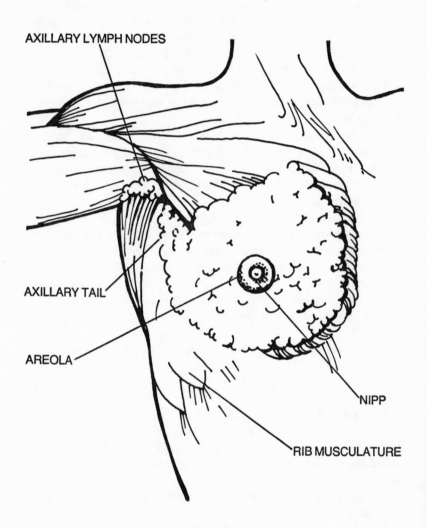

AXILLARY LYMPH NODES

AXILLARY TAIL

AREOLA

NIPP

RIB MUSCULATURE

THE AXILLARY TAIL OF THE BREAST

A drawing of the breast and chest wall, with the skin (but not the nipple) removed. Note the "axillary tail" of breast tissue extending toward the axilla. There are more axillary nodes under the large pectoral muscles that support the breast.

tissue. Further careful examination into this mass of tissue will show that it is organized into lobes, like sections of an orange. There are perhaps twelve to twenty-one such lobes each containing a duct system. The outermost portion of the duct system is thin and finely branched. It might be helpful to compare this microscopic duct structure to the outermost, finest branches of a delicate plant. The fine ducts converge and form large ducts which run toward the nipple, much as the main stems of the plant go toward the ground. Ultimately, at least one duct from each lobe comes to the nipple. Thus, milk from any part of the breast has a pathway to the nipple.

Looking further at this mass of breast material with skin removed, the arteries and veins become identifiable. (See figure 14, page 166) There is no point in your knowing the arteries and veins by name, but as you can see from the illustration, the breast has an abundant blood supply.

The breast has an equally abundant network called *lymphatic vessels*. These vessels carry lymph fluid. Lymphatic vessels are microscopic tubules that permeate the entire breast (and virtually the entire body). In the breast, the vessels are interconnected. They function in the breast by carrying lymph fluid away from the breast. The clear lymph fluid contains white blood cells that function to destroy bacteria. (The white blood cells also have a limited ability to fight cancer cells.)

The lymph fluid is carried away from the breast to *lymph nodes*. The lymph nodes are organized filter stations of white blood cells, and prevent bacteria from entering the bloodstream.

Bacteria and foreign material are prevented from entering the bloodstream by the filtering action of the lymph nodes. Doctors often refer to this whole system of lymphatic vessels and lymph nodes associated with the breast as the *lymphatic drainage of the breast.*

If you have ever had a cold or sore throat and have felt painful swellings in your neck, you have experienced lymph nodes in action. In response to the infection in your throat, the lymph

Figure 14

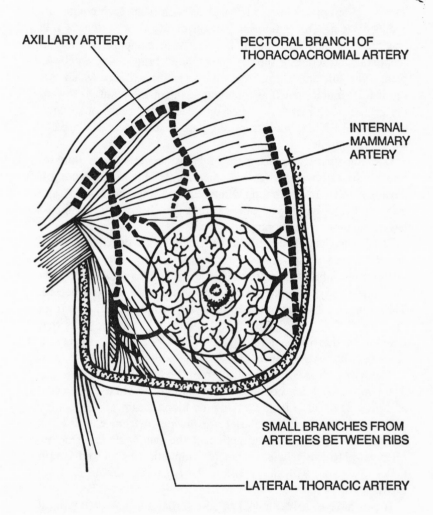

AXILLARY ARTERY

PECTORAL BRANCH OF
THORACOACROMIAL ARTERY

INTERNAL
MAMMARY
ARTERY

SMALL BRANCHES FROM
ARTERIES BETWEEN RIBS

LATERAL THORACIC ARTERY

THE BLOOD SUPPLY OF THE BREAST

The blood supply of the breast. The blood vessels represented by
dotted lines are those which are behind the muscles of the chest and,
in the case of the internal mammary artery, the ribs.

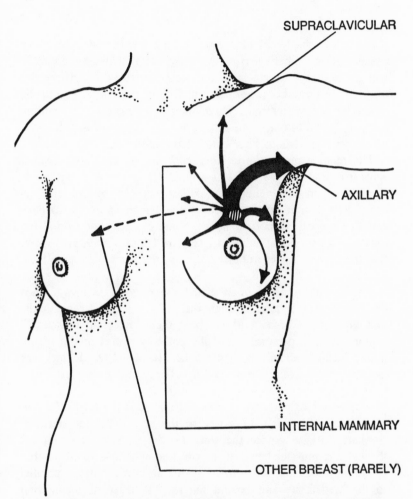

Figure 15

SUPRACLAVICULAR

AXILLARY

INTERNAL MAMMARY

OTHER BREAST (RARELY)

LYMPHATIC ROUTES FOR THE SPREAD OF BREAST CANCER
A schematic diagram showing the different possible lymphatic pathways by which a cancer may spread. The pathway to the axillary
nodes is shown by a wide arrow because this is the most important
route of spread. The supraclavicular and internal mammary routes
are shown by narrower solid lines. A possible pathway of spread to
the other breast is indicated by a dotted line, as this is a rare course
of lymphatic spread, while the other three are common.

nodes, fighting to keep the bacteria from spreading to other parts of your body, have swollen with additional white blood cells and have become painful.

Since it is the lymphatic vessels of the breast that often carry cancer cells to other parts of the body, the first place the cancer will go from the breast is to the local lymph nodes. There the cancer may grow because of an inability of the white blood cells to destroy the cancer cells. Three main pathways can lead cancer-carrying lymph to one of the three principal groups of lymph nodes whose purpose it is to filter lymph from the breast.

The main route is the *axillary pathway,* appropriately named since it drains into the axilla or armpit. (If you look at figure 15, page 167, you can identify the axillary pathway by the wide arrow.) The lymph nodes that filter the lymph from the axillary pathway are called *axillary nodes.* Some of them are behind the muscles that support the breasts. (Figure 16, page 169, also shows that the axillary nodes are often close to the veins that come from the arm.)

The second route is often called the *pectoral pathway,* since the lymph vessels pass through the main muscles, or pectorals, that support the breasts. More about these important muscles in a moment. The pectoral lymphatic pathway drains to the lymph nodes located above the collarbone. Incidentally, doctors are fond of calling collarbones *clavicles.* These nodes, located above the clavicles, are called *supraclavicular nodes.*

A third major pathway of lymph drainage is the *internal mammary pathway,* which flows toward the breastbone, or sternum. A short distance before the sternum, the pathway goes inward through the muscles between the ribs and ends in a small number of lymph nodes that are situated beside an artery running parallel to the breastbone and behind the ribs. Because of its internal location, and because it supplies blood to the breast, this artery is called the *internal mammary artery.* Logic in nomenclature continues to prevail: Since the lymph nodes are near this artery, they are called *internal mammary nodes.*

Figure 16

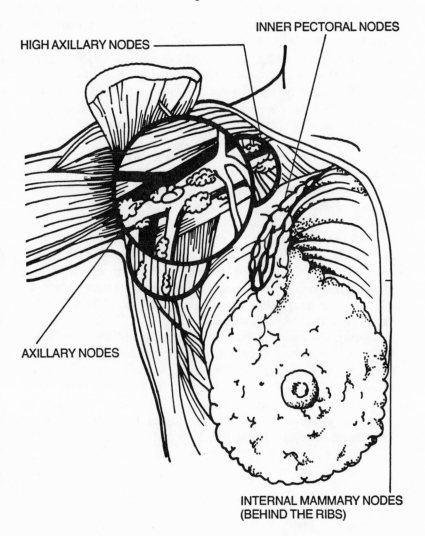

HIGH AXILLARY NODES

INNER PECTORAL NODES

AXILLARY NODES

INTERNAL MAMMARY NODES
(BEHIND THE RIBS)

THE AXILLARY LYMPH NODES

An anatomic drawing in which the skin has been removed and the pectoralis muscles have been cut and pulled back. With the aid of magnification (the circles) one can see the axillary nodes. The internal mammary nodes lie behind the chest wall.

These three different groups of nodes are dealt with in varying ways if they are thought to harbor cancer. The axillary nodes are often removed. The supraclavicular and internal mammary nodes are frequently treated by radiation and/or chemotherapy.

It is interesting that there are vague and variable interconnections between the lymphatic vessels of one breast and those of the opposite breast. Occasionally, cancer can travel to the opposite breast by this interconnecting pathway, but fortunately this happens rarely.

You will remember that the muscles supporting the breast are also important. The breast is supported by the *pectoralis major* and the *pectoralis minor* muscles. They are differentiated by name because of their size—the pectoralis major being the larger of the two. The pectoralis major lies on top of the pectoralis minor (as you can see in figure 17, page 173). These muscles are used in a variety of motions of the arm at the shoulder joint. Because there are lymph nodes hidden behind and between these two muscles, they are often removed in surgery for breast cancer. It takes no great imagination to understand that loss of these muscles causes considerable physical problems.

So, then, the basic anatomy of the breast is not all that difficult. What you must come away with here is an understanding of these structures of the breast and what they do: the fat and connective tissue, the milk ducts, the blood supply, the lymphatic vessels and lymph nodes, and the important muscles that support the breast.

Having understood that, the next thing to consider is what happens when cancer develops in the breast.

3. The Unpleasant Facts About Untreated Breast Cancer

Amputating a breast, giving large doses of radiation, or administering dangerous and toxic drugs are not things doctors undertake lightly. They are actions that must be prompted by critical considerations. Such drastic steps are taken because doctors and patients are dealing with a very serious disease, and in trying to cure cancer disease, doctors often have to resort to hazardous types of therapy.

To understand how serious a disease breast cancer can be, we must enter a brutal and unpleasant discussion. We must ask the question, "What happens to the patient if no treatment is given?" We must know how the disease arises, exacerbates, spreads, incapacitates, and kills.

The untreated course of a disease is referred to as its *natural history*. If the natural history of breast cancer were to be described in two words, they would be "unpredictable" and "grim." Indeed, cancer of the breast is more unpredictable than any other cancers except malignant melanoma.

Breast cancer often arises from the cells that line the milk ducts. It is uncertain at present whether only a single cell undergoes a malignant change or whether several cells in a particular area undergo this change at the same time. In becoming malignant, recall that the cells undergo the following changes:

—They divide and keep on dividing relentlessly.
—They assume to a varying degree a different appearance from the cells from which they came.
—Along with the changes in appearance, they lose to a varying degree their ability to perform the functions of the tissue from which they came.
—As they grow, they have a tendency to invade and destroy distant areas of the body. This phenomenon is known as metastasis.

The causes of this malignant transformation of cells are basically unknown, and are the subject of widespread debate and confusion. Many experts now feel that there are multiple factors interplaying to cause breast cancer.

The controversy surrounding the causes of breast cancer remains lively and unresolved. Most important here is that you come away from this book with an understanding of the *known* factors that increase your risk of breast cancer.

A breast cancer starts as a microscopic growing mass of abnormal cells. It is now believed that cancer cells divide at a steady rate. The average length of time necessary for all the cells in a tumor to divide has been designated as the *doubling time*. With the passage of one doubling time, the number of cells in the mass is doubled and the weight of the mass is doubled. Since the cancer starts as a single cell, or small mass of cells, it must go through many doubling times before it reaches a size that can be detected. The doubling time for a breast cancer has been estimated to range from 6 to 540 days, with an average of 105 days. Thus, cancer may be present in a breast for many years before it is detectable.

A one-centimeter mass (about the size of your fingertip) is usually the smallest size that can be detected by palpation (feel-

Figure 17

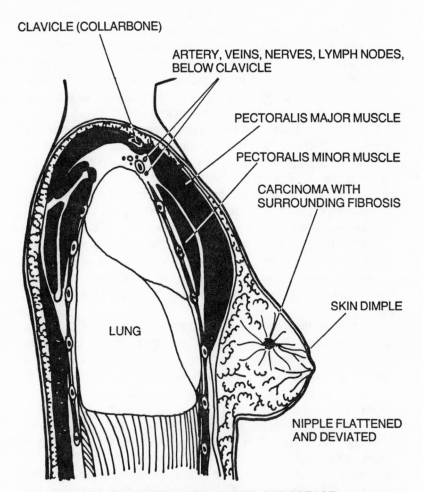

CLAVICLE (COLLARBONE)

ARTERY, VEINS, NERVES, LYMPH NODES, BELOW CLAVICLE

PECTORALIS MAJOR MUSCLE

PECTORALIS MINOR MUSCLE

CARCINOMA WITH SURROUNDING FIBROSIS

SKIN DIMPLE

LUNG

NIPPLE FLATTENED AND DEVIATED

CROSS-SECTION OF A CANCEROUS BREAST
Cross-section of the breast with a cancer in it. Notice the tumor with its strands radiating out in all directions. This is the so-called "stellate" pattern of growth frequently exhibited by cancers. Also notice the pectoralis muscles: behind them and below the clavicle lie the axillary lymph nodes along with a number of nerves, arteries, and veins. Notice also that the growth of the tumor has caused changes in the overlying skin—dimpling of the skin, for example, and flattening and deviation of the nipple.

ing the breast); it is called an *early cancer,* but biologically, it is rather far along in its course. A one-centimeter mass contains over a million cells. It has undergone approximately thirty doubling times. After forty-two or forty-three doubling times, the average patient is dead. Thus, an early cancer has gone through two-thirds to three-fourths of its natural history when it is first discovered. It needs only to undergo relatively few more doubling times before the woman has massive disease.

The cancer originating in the breast is referred to as the *primary tumor.* If left alone, the primary tumor will continue to grow. It infiltrates along the milk ducts, connective tissue strands, and the mammary fat. This pattern of infiltration causes the cancer to take on an irregular or stellate shape. (See xeromammogram, end papers) As it grows, it begins to invade other structures such as the skin and chest wall. It also invades the lymphatic vessels and the blood vessels, thus setting the stage for distant spread of the cancer. Invasion of the skin gives rise to a number of the signs of the presence of malignancy, such as dimpling of the skin, firmness, puckering, or turning inward of the nipple (see figure 17, page 173).

Usually, if the cancer remains untreated, the overlying skin will be invaded. It will first become stuck to the underlying tumor, and soon will become firm, swollen, and red. After a variable period of time the skin is destroyed and an ulceration occurs. The ulcer enlarges and deepens relentlessly. A patient suffering from this problem is a sad sight. An ulcerated tumor is often a rotten, infected, foul-smelling mass, exuding pus and bleeding easily. A patient in this condition, if she is not in a coma, is thoroughly miserable. The deeper portions of the tumor may ultimately invade the chest wall and cause pain and fixation of the mass to the chest wall. Usually, by the time ulceration has occurred, the mass has invaded the chest wall unless the breast is extremely large. (Remember, I have been describing advanced disease.)

At some point the disease begins to spread from the primary

lesion to other sites of the body, causing metastasis of the regional lymph nodes. This is very common. The regional lymph nodes, as mentioned earlier, are the *axillary,* the *supraclavicular,* and the *internal mammary nodes.* It has been stated that if a malignant lump has been palpable in a breast for only one month, the axillary nodes will contain cancer in 50 percent of the cases. If the lump has been palpable for six months, the axilliary nodes will contain cancer in a higher percent of the cases. (See figure 15, page 167).

It should be emphasized, however, that spread to other organs can occur *even* before spread to the lymph nodes. This is one phenomenon that helps explain why breast cancer is such an unpredictable disease.

The reasons for this phenomenon of early spread to distant organs are not totally understood. It is thought that malignant cells floating in the lymph sometimes pass right through the lymph nodes without being stopped. Also, a cancer may erode into a vein, giving the cancer direct access to the bloodstream. Not all cancer cells that get into the bloodstream develop cancers elsewhere, but some do. Once the disease is widespread in the body, it is considered incurable by all present-day methods of treatment, although advances are being made through the use of high doses of powerful drugs—chemotherapy.

Recent news of promising chemotherapy advances has come from Italy as well as from the USA. More and more doctors are treating breast cancer patients immediately after surgery with drugs, some of which are a combination of five. Some, as in the Italian study, use three drugs.

It is important to note that these studies are still very young. The results should be considered with caution, since at present the effect of these drugs on survival, and their possible long-term side effects, are unknown. However, early data seems to indicate that progress is being made in the area of breast cancer treatment.

Lymphatic spread manifests itself in the axilla as masses that are usually firm and nontender. At first, the disease is contained within the lymph nodes, but as the metastases grow they break out of the capsules surrounding the lymph nodes and invade the surrounding area, just as the primary tumor may be doing. As invasion of the axilla progresses, these metastases become immobile. The axilla may ultimately fill with cancer. This can be extremely painful.

The disease spreads to other organs of the body directly through the bloodstream or via the lymphatics, which ultimately drain into the bloodstream. At this stage the disease is often found in multiple organs. The most frequent sites of distant metastases found at autopsy are, in order of descending frequency, the lungs, the pleura (the membrane that covers the lungs), bones, the liver, the adrenal glands, skin at other sites, the brain, and the ovaries. These are by no means the only sites that can be involved.

Unpleasant as it might be, you should understand how metastasis to these areas may affect the body. It is important to realize that cases vary a great deal and that not every patient will suffer all of these problems during the remainder of her life.

It is also important to know that at least partially effective treatments for those severe problems associated with breast cancer are now available. However, once the patient has distant metastasis, she is almost always incurable.

Lung metastases may present themselves as multiple nodular densities that can be seen as "snowballs" on a chest X ray. Occasionally only a single nodule is seen. The nodular types of metastases cause the patient remarkably little harm until they have grown quite large, unless they are associated with metastases of the pleura (the membrane covering of the lung). After they are large, they may cause coughing and shortness of breath. Another much common form of pulmonary metastases is the so-called lymphangitic type. The lungs are diffusely, bilaterally, involved by cancer—which is to say that the lungs are totally permeated with tumor. The most prominent symptom is shortness of breath, which rapidly worsens. The patient soon chokes to death.

Pleural metastases are involvements of the membranes covering the lungs. Such metastases develop sooner or later in the majority of patients with lung metastases. In some patients, pleural metastases cause pain on deep breathing. Collections of fluid in the pleural space—the area between the lung and the chest wall—may form. This accumulation of fluid is called a *pleural effusion,* and if massive, may cause death.

If the bones are invaded by the breast cancer, they are attacked at multiple sites. Bone metastases can be classified as belonging to one of the two clinically significant kinds.

1. Osteolytic (or bone-destroying). An X ray of a bone affected by an osteolytic metastasis will show an area in which the bone has been destroyed by the cancer. This type of bone metastasis is far more commonly found in cases of breast cancer than the second type of bone metastasis, namely—

2. Osteoblastic (or "bone forming"). An X ray of a bone affected by an osteoblastic metastasis will show increased density of the bone at the site of the lesion. The cancer has, in some poorly understood fashion, caused a local increase in bone formation. This type of bone metastasis is very uncommon in cases of breast cancer.

Bone metastases can cause three major problems. The first is pain, and it is often severe. The second is fractures, due to the erosion of the bones by the osteolytic kind of metastases. The fractures are painful. If the bone is weight-bearing, such as the femur, the patient is unable to walk. If the metastases involve several bones in the spine, it may collapse. This can damage the spinal cord and cause paralysis below the level of the collapse. Finally, bone destruction leads to an elevated level of calcium in the blood called *hypercalcemia.* Untreated severe hypercalcemia often leads to rapid death, which is thought to be due to cardiac arrest.

Liver metastases usually produce few if any symptoms until an advanced stage is reached. The liver may become so large as to cause abdominal distress. If bile ducts of the liver are obstructed by tumor, jaundice develops and causes itching.

Adrenal metastases, kidney metastases, and *ovarian metastases* are grouped together because they usually cause few problems for the patients. Few patients develop overt symptoms until the cancer is advanced.

Brain metastases cause headache, nausea, vomiting, visual disturbances, convulsive seizures, and death. The untreated patient progresses rather rapidly toward death.

Skin metastases cause superficial lumps that may ulcerate in time.

In addition to the specific effects referable to these organs, there are the generalized systemic effects of cancer. One of these is the so-called *cachexia of malignancy*. The patient loses her appetite, will not eat, gradually becomes emaciated. There is also what is referred to as the "anemia of cancer," which is often seen in cancer patients with widespread disease. In this condition the patient develops a moderate-to-severe anemia that cannot be corrected unless the cancer is brought under control or transfusions are given. It has been shown that this anemia is caused by a profound disturbance in iron metabolism. Exactly how the cancer causes this disturbance is not known.

These are by no means all of the possible ways the disease manifests itself. Many other less frequent problems are possible.

All these grim words add up to the fact that the patient with *untreated* breast cancer suffers from both local and distant problems owing to the progression of her disease. In time, one or several of these problems will ultimately kill her.

The time from the onset of problems to that of death can be thought of as the natural duration of the disease. These days it is uncommon to encounter a patient who has had a breast cancer that has been totally untreated. However, data on such patients exists. In 1962 a doctor retrospectively analyzed the records of 250 patients with untreated breast cancer who were admitted to Britain's Middlesex Cancer Charity Hospital between 1805 and

1933. They were generally patients with advanced disease who came to the hospital to die. In his group of patients the median survival was 2.7 years.

There was, however, a great range of variation in duration of survival. For that reason I want to repeat that breast cancer is highly unpredictable. In a few of the patients the disease ran its course in three months. At the other end of the scale, one woman in this Middlesex series survived untreated for nineteen years.

There is also this to consider: Part of the prognosis of breast cancer seems to lie in the so-called inherent biological nature of the tumor, which means that some tumors seem to be more aggressive than others. Regardless of the method of treatment, there are *no laws concerning cancer,* and since different cancers behave in different ways, the reasonable if unsettling assumption, therefore, is that specific tumors may spread *at any stage of their evolution.* Breast cancer may spread to practically any part of the body.

4.   The Types of Breast Cancer

We have just emerged from a long, sometimes complicated, and all too often unpleasant consideration of how breast cancer can affect the body, especially if nothing is done about it.

Until now, breast cancer has been treated as singular—one disease. Prepare yourself for another unpleasantness: breast cancer is many diseases. Aware of this, doctors determine the general type of cancer by examining the suspicious tissue microscopically. The cells and their pattern differ from type to type, although the differences are often extremely subtle.

These distinctions are of more than academic interest. They can mean big differences in how patients are treated. More important, the type of cancer can influence the patient's chances for survival. Clearly then, accurate diagnosis can at times mean the difference between life and death. In other instances it can mean the difference between radical surgery, with its attendant deformity, and more simple and less deforming surgery.

Some types of breast cancer are associated with a better prognosis; others with a worse one. Some grow faster and spread earlier than others. Of course, the extent to which the disease has advanced at the moment of discovery and treatment is very significant in considering the chance for cure of any given patient.

181

To help diagnose and differentiate the types of breast cancer, we will now introduce the medical specialist known to all of us as the pathologist.

Although the pathologist does not perform surgery, prescribe shots and pills, although he (or she) does not usually walk the hospital halls telling patients what lovely flowers their relatives have sent, he is one of the most important doctors in the team taking care of cancer patients.

The responsibility for making the correct diagnosis rests largely on his shoulders. A wrong diagnosis can mean disaster—a fact he knows all too well. Obviously, the fates of many people he may never even see can depend on the accuracy of his diagnosis. Indeed, most hospitals stipulate that any tissue removed from the patient must be examined by the pathologist.

He is the doctor who will examine the specimen or lump removed from a woman's breast. He must determine what a particular tissue is. Is it benign? If so, what sort of benign disease is it? Is it malignant? If so, what kind of malignancy is it? These are just some of the questions the pathologist must resolve. The answers are not easy. For this reason, he has spent four to five years in formal training in his specialty after graduation from medical school.

Pathological study of a specimen under consideration is generally regarded as the most definitive means of diagnosis. The doctor treating the patient has often already made a tentative clinical diagnosis, but it must await confirmation by the pathologist.

To construct his report, the pathologist must first use his extensive knowledge of pathology and, most importantly, his experience. If he is to diagnose cancer, such diagnosis must be unmistakable. If there is any doubt, he should seek consultation with others in his field.

A diagnosis is a carefully considered opinion. It depends on many variables, all of approximately equal weight. First, the tissue specimen must be adequate and it must be prepared carefully for microscopic examination. Often, and unfortunately, the pathologist has very little tissue to work with. Perhaps he has only a collection of cells the size of a grain of rice, or a long, pencil-lead-thin sliver of tissue from a needle biopsy; perhaps he has tissue from an area that is not entirely representative of the tumor as a whole. Clearly, he can make no decision or diagnosis that is any better than the tissue on which it is based. The pathologist must be open and honest, and make this as clear as possible to the doctors who are taking care of the patient.

Much like the quality of the tissue collected, the pathologist himself is also a variable. He is a human being, and not always able to provide a definitive answer despite his knowledge and experience. A pathologist must be given time to examine the slide carefully, and possibly more time to refer to his collection of slides and books. If a surgeon rushes a pathologist into a decision concerning suspicious tissue, and the pathologist has had insufficient time to evaluate that tissue properly, a surgical procedure based on ignorance is risked. In other words, the tissue may have been suspicious and typical of cancer, but not clearly diagnostic of cancer. There have been some tragic cases in which breasts that were originally thought to contain cancer were removed and later found not to contain cancer. The lesson is plain: The pathologist should not be rushed into a decision. If any doubt exists, further study of the tissue should be performed. More intensive study can be done by another pathologist, more slides can be made from the suspicious tissue, or a repeat biopsy can even be performed. "Probability" and "likelihood" are not words surgeons should ever seek to elicit from pathologists. You can always request the opinion of another pathologist. In fact, it is often advisable to have a second opinion from another source.

If these cautionary words seem all too remote, here are the facts of a recent case to argue to the contrary.

A forty-five-year-old woman appeared in the tumor clinic of a large hospital with what seemed to be the clinical signs of a rare and devastating breast cancer called inflammatory carcinoma.

Most patients with this form of cancer die within two years no matter how it is treated. The tissue obtained was not adequate for the surgical pathologist to give a clear-cut decision on whether or not the tissue was indeed cancerous. The pathologist asked the surgeon for a second biopsy. The surgeon then took a tissue specimen from a part of the breast farther from the inflamed area, but unfortunately this specimen contained a great deal of fatty tissue from which it was impossible to make a diagnosis. The pathologist had therefore to be frank and insisted on making two requests of the surgeon. He asked the surgeon to wait for a permanent pathology report to be completed and he asked him for a third biopsy to supply him with a small amount of the skin to determine if it was microscopically consistent with this type of breast cancer.

The patient did prove to have a malignancy, but it was not the dreaded inflammatory cancer first suspected.

This scrupulous procedure took courage on the part of the pathologist, for he was faced with a demanding surgeon who wanted a quick decision. The result was, however, to the patient's benefit. The doctors did not have to give her a "perhaps only two years to live" prognosis and they were able to set out to help her with an accurate diagnosis in hand.

Having viewed, however briefly, a pathologist's task, and having noted its importance, it is time to return to a familiar situation. A lump is found in a woman's breast. What is it? We are reassured by the reminder that the odds say three out of four lumps are not cancerous. However, the only way to be sure is by a biopsy and the tissue examined under the microscope by the pathologist. This process by looking at the tissue with the microscope is called *histologic examination.*

If the lump is not cancer, the pathologist may be confronted by one of the two main types of benign disease.

The lump most commonly seen under the microscope in women under thirty is called a *fibroadenoma,* so called because it has both fibrous and glandular parts. When felt in a breast, it is a solid discrete lump, usually smooth and regular, single and not tender. Although fibroadenomas are generally thought not to be premalignant tumors leading to cancer, most doctors feel it is wise to remove them because of the possibility that they may grow, and cause pain and deformity. Their surgical removal is usually a simple procedure.

Cysts are the other most common lumps found most frequently in women aged thirty to menopause. A cyst is most apt to be filled with fluid and often can be drained in the doctor's office with a needle (aspiration of fluid). These cysts may be multiple or solitary and are frequently painful. It is important to realize that if no fluid is obtained from a suspected cyst, or if a lump persists, it must be biopsied.

It is also important to remember that if a woman has a history of fibroadenomas or cysts, their having been benign once or twice is no guarantee that another lump found in her breast will be benign as well.

Chronic cystic disease is frequently confused with carcinoma of the breast. It is often painful, particularly before and during the menstrual period. The cysts are often multiple in number and usually are found in both breasts. These lumps should be biopsied if they enlarge enough to be felt. The woman should be followed carefully by her doctor and examined at properly timed intervals. Occasionally a woman's breasts may be so painful all the time that a *bilateral subcutaneous mastectomy* is advised (with breast implants at the time of surgery) to relieve the pain. This form of surgery is also used when the woman must face constant repeated biopsies. A plastic surgeon who is familiar with this procedure should be sought out. Owing to the current controversy about silicone-bag breast implants, it seems advisable to take advantage of the soft inflatable breast implants.

In addition to these two major types of benign diseases, there are several signs and symptoms that, although feared by many women as sure signs of cancer, usually have benign origins. One is bloody discharge from the nipple, often caused by a benign lump called a *papilloma*. It is a wartlike tumor, the size of a pinhead, which obstructs the mammary ducts. The bleeding, however, may sometimes be the sign of cancer. Thus a biopsy is warranted.

Skin irritation or itching of the central breast or nipple is often due to allergy or a nervous condition. It may, however, be the first signs of *Paget's disease* of the nipple, a rare form of breast cancer that affects the central ducts and overlying skin.

Breast pain and tenderness during a woman's menstrual period are usually not indicative of breast cancer. Women taking birth control pills often experience pain, tenderness, or enlargement in both breasts. These are common reactions to the estrogens in the pill. To date there is no evidence that birth control pills lead to breast cancer. A recent study, however, shows that taking birth control pills may protect the breast from "benign breast disease" such as fibrocystic disease.

Suppose, though, the lump that the pathologist is examining is not benign but malignant. What kinds of cancer might he find? Further, what is the significance of each type to both the patient and the doctor?

Here we must use medical jargon. Cancers are recognized and identified according to classifications developed over a number of years by several eminent specialists in the field. Happily, it is not important that you remember the names. What is important, however, is that you know there are differences between one breast cancer and another and that these differences can be significant. Bear with the names, even be amused or awed by them if so they affect you, but by all means pay some attention to the significance of each.

TYPE ONE—*Nonmetastasizing (Noninvasive)*. You will probably surmise from the title that this cancer has a good prognosis. It stays within the milk duct and does not tend to spread to other parts of the body. Because of this, radical surgery is almost never needed to cure this tumor. Unfortunately, less than 10 percent of breast cancers are of this type. The name of the cancer that comprises Type One is *comedo carcinoma without stromal invasion.*

TYPE TWO—*Rarely Metastasizing (Invasive).* As you can gather from the words used to classify this type, these cancers are said to metastasize (spread to distant areas of the body) only rarely. That's the good news. You already know the bad news: These tumors invade locally and thus cause a great deal of trouble, as you will recall from the earlier description of how breast cancer affects the body. It is logical, then, that the treatment of these tumors must be more aggressive than that of Type One. The names of the tumors found in this type: *pure extracellular mucinous or colloid carcinoma; medullary carcinomas with lymphocytic infiltration; well-differentiated adenocarcinomas.* There is absolutely no hope of translating these names into real English. If you *must* know, see your friendly neighborhood pathologist.

TYPE THREE—*Moderately Metastasizing (Always Invasive).* Again, from the name of the type some accurate deductions follow more or less easily. These are more serious cancers than the first two types. Not only do they invade, but they spread to distant parts of the body. The names of tumors in this type are: *adenocarcinoma* (a cancer that originates in cells that form glands) and *infiltrating ductal carcinoma.* The latter deserves special attention because it is the single one most commonly found. As its name proclaims, it originates in the cells that line the milk ducts and it grows by infiltrating its way through the breast. Of course, it can also spread to distant parts of the body. Aggressive treatment is warranted for this type of cancer.

TYPE FOUR—*Highly Metastasizing (Always Invasive).* Sounds bad and it is. Fortunately this type of cancer is encountered infrequently. When a patient has Type Four, her doctors need to be particularly alert to signs that it has spread to other parts of her body. The name of cancer that fits into this category is *undifferentiated carcinoma.* This is a cancer whose cells are so abnormal-looking that the pathologist cannot tell for sure—or even guess—what type of cells they were before they became malignant.

In addition to the different types of cancer included in this classification, there are a couple of others worth mentioning. Already mentioned is *inflammatory carcinoma,* a rare and deadly cancer considered by some doctors to be diagnosable solely on clinical evidence, specifically diffuse swelling firmness, and redness of the skin and breast. At most medical centers, however, the staff seems to agree that widespread filling with cancer of the lymphatic vessels just below the skin has to be demonstrated by the pathologist before this diagnosis is made. (In other words, the pathologist also needs a sample of the skin.)

Inflammatory carcinoma is one cancer in which radical mastectomy—indeed, any breast surgery other than biopsy—is not indicated. This is because over the years it has been found that patients with this disease die faster if they have sugery than if they do not. Surgery in this instance seems to spread the cancer. (Incidentally, a breast that has been injected with liquid silicone may in time develop an appearance that is clinically indistinguishable from inflammatory carcinoma—all the more reason for a skin and tissue sample to be taken to the pathologist.)

Finally, there is such a thing as cancer of the male breast. It is a rare disease, but one more deadly type by type than cancer of the female breast.

5. The Stages of Breast Cancer

After the type of cancer present in the breast has been determined, the logical step is to ask the question: How much cancer is present and where is it located?

The answers are at least as important as awareness of what type of cancer is present. Indeed, for many patients the answer to these questions are even more important than identifying the type of cancer. For example, a woman with breast cancer that has spread to her body should not be subjected to a radical surgery, since the operation offers no chance for her to be cured. Other forms of therapy such as chemotherapy should be used.

This process of determining the extent of the cancer and its location is called *cancer staging*. In staging a patient's cancer, doctors try to determine the following: the characteristics of the primary (original) tumor—What is its size? Its location? What are the surrounding structures it has invaded? They seek to find out through the process of staging whether or not the lymph nodes have been involved, and if so how much cancer they contain. Also, of extreme importance is whether or not the cancer has spread to other parts of the body. These are the vital preliminary questions. After the doctor has found his answers he can stage the patient and assign her to one of four groups.

Well and good, but how does this process act to help the patient and the doctor? First, it helps the doctor in planning the patient's treatment. It gives him some idea of her prognosis. It assists him in evaluating the results of his work. In other words, at some later time he can go back to his records and seek conclusions that may help him and other doctors to treat future patients. Indeed, this is one of the methods by which many medical discoveries have been made. Finally, staging helps doctors in communicating to one another about patients and the results of various treatments.

The following is a commonly used clinical staging system in this country. It was developed with consideration of the benefits mentioned above.

There are more precise and therefore more complicated systems. but this is a translation of the one developed by the American Joint Committee on Cancer Staging and it will suffice for our needs:

STAGE ONE: *Palpable tumor in the breast; no palpable axillary lymph nodes; distant metastases not suspected.* (Here, the doctor believes the cancer is located in the breast alone.)

STAGE TWO: *Palpable tumor in the breast; palpable axillary lymph nodes; no metastasis to these nodes is suspected; distant metastasis is not suspected.* (Here, the doctor can feel enlarged lymph nodes in the axilla and he believes the enlargement is not due to cancer. He does not suspect the disease has spread to the rest of the patient's body.)

STAGE THREE: *Palpable tumor in the breast; tumor fixed; infiltration; ulceration or thickening of the skin of the breast by the tumor or invasion of the pectoral muscle or attachment of the tumor to the chest wall; usually there are palpable lymph nodes; distant metastasis is not suspected.* (This is simply more extensive disease of the breast and axillary lymph nodes than

in Stage Two, but still the cancer is not thought to have spread
to the rest of the body.)

STAGE FOUR: *Palpable tumor in the breast; distant metastasis.*
(The cancer has invaded the rest of the body. What's important is that the disease has spread to a distant part of the body,
for example, the liver. A Stage Four patient is usually incurable
by present methods. However, it is possible to keep the cancer
under control for a long period of time in some patients.)

You have probably surmised that the more advanced the case,
the worse the prognosis. Stages One and Two are generally treated
by surgery. A Stage One tumor is the most treatable. Stage Three
tumors are less treatable. The patient with widespread cancer is
not usually curable.

Be aware that this is a "clinical staging system"—that is, the
patient's clinical stage is determined by what the doctor can see
and feel, plus evidence gathered from X rays and tests. Bone scans,
liver scans, and a chest X ray are made. A battery of blood tests
is needed to evaluate the enzyme status of the liver, check the
blood count, etc. The results of these tests can often indicate the
spread of cancer.

A scan of any sort essentially means introducing weak radioactive material into the bloodstream. The material is taken up by
the body. A machine resembling an X ray moves over the areas
of suspicion and makes a series of photographs. Deposits of cancer may show up either as areas of increased radioactivity or as
areas of decreased radioactivity, depending on the type of scan
being made. Many other conditions and normal variations can at
times mimic cancer on radioisotope scans such as these, so it takes
great skill to interpret them properly. Scans can be very valuable,
however, in the overall assessment of a patient. Even if they are
normal, a set of scans—at least a liver and bone scan—can provide what is known as a "baseline" for future comparison. Often
the change noticed in a scan picture, when a scan is repeated, is

the most significant piece of information about a patient's status. To detect this change, a newly made scan is compared with the original ones.

Staging a patient, using all the available means, is an *absolute must before any treatment*—surgical or otherwise—is begun. The scans and blood tests are also known as a *metastatic workup*. In other words, checking the body for distant cancer. These tests should be used if there is a diagnosis of cancer or if a very high suspicion of cancer is present—before any treatment is begun.

Thus, it is possible to incorrectly stage a patient. Often, distant cancer is simply too small to detect by present techniques. Also, findings may be present that suggest widespread cancer, but these findings may be caused by some nonmalignant process. In addition, you should know that there are many noncancerous causes of enlarged axillary nodes; for example, a chronically infected fingernail. Factors such as these are responsible for errors in staging.

Despite these uncertainties, it is still absolutely necessary for the doctor and the patient to assess the situation as thoroughly as they can before any treatment is begun. The more known about a patient before any treatment is initiated, the less chance of error and the greater the chances are of applying proper therapy for the best result.

Glossary

Words and Phrases You Need to Know

Areola. The circle of pigmented skin that surrounds the nipple.

Axilla. The armpit. More specifically, the area that is above the lungs and the rib cage but below and behind the collarbone. This area contains blood vessels, nerves, and the axillary lymph nodes to which breast cancer commonly spreads.

Benign. Not malignant.

Biopsy. The removal of a piece of tissue for examination by the pathologist. A tumor may be removed totally in a biopsy—an excisional biopsy—or a part of the tumor may be cut out—an incisional biopsy.

Cancer. A disease state in which the body cells have become abnormal and have gained the capacity to damage the body. These cells differ from normal cells in the following ways: they grow "autonomously," that is, in an independent and unrestrained fashion; they appear abnormal under the microscope and have lost the ability to perform their original functions; they have the capacity to invade new body structures and to spread to distant parts of the body. Because the body has many different kinds of cells, there are many different kinds of cancer. The major types of cancer that affect the breast are listed on pages 181-188.

Chemotherapy. Chemotherapy, or cancer chemotherapy, is the

193

treatment of cancer with drugs that have the ability to destroy tumors or block their growth. Chemotherapy is usually reserved for patients with advanced cancer in whom surgery and/or radiation therapy have failed or will fail. This is because, so far, no chemotherapy has been proven to cure breast cancer patients, and the drugs that are presently used are dangerous and often have severe side effects. One exception to the statement that chemotherapy is reserved for advanced cases, however, is in the area of "adjuvant chemotherapy." Studies are under way in which an anticancer drug is given to patients soon after surgery for breast cancer—an "adjuvant," or aid to surgery. The purpose of this therapy is, hopefully, to eradicate any small deposits of tumor that may be present in the body after surgery. To date the results have been encouraging in terms of preventing recurrence of the disease after surgery. However, it is too soon to tell whether this form of treatment will withstand the test of time.

Cancer staging. This is the process in which doctors determine how much cancer is present in the body and where it is located. The degree of advancement of the disease is referred to as its "stage."

Cystic disease. Cystic disease, also known as "fibrocystic disease" or "mammary dysplasia," is the most important cause of benign lumps found in the breasts of women from the age of thirty to the time of their menopause. Remember that three out of four breast lumps will prove to be benign.

Duct. A tube which can carry secretions. In the breast, milk ducts carry milk. Significantly, a milk duct is frequently the site in which breast cancer arises.

Epidemiology. The study of disease patterns and their spread.

Estrogen. A female hormone that is produced by the ovaries. This hormone is at least partially responsible for many of the bodily characteristics of women, such as larger breasts than men, a higher-pitched voice, and different distribution of body fat.

Fibroadenoma. A benign breast lump that has both fibrous and glandular parts. This type of lump is the most frequent cause of breast masses in women under thirty. Again, remember that three out of four breast lumps will prove to be benign.

Frozen section. This is a quick method the surgical pathologist uses to determine whether or not a tumor is cancerous. Diagnosis with this method is used when the surgeon has planned a "one-stage procedure." (See "one-stage treatment"). This is a suboptimal method of making up a pathological diagnosis, for there are many sources of possible error owing to the speed with which the tissue is processed.

General anesthetic. A form of anesthesia, or pain relief, that involves putting the patient to sleep. It is more dangerous and more expensive for the patient than the "local method of anesthesia." (See "local anesthetic")

Hormone therapy. In the instance of breast cancer, this is treatment of the disease by giving the patient certain types of hormones. This form of therapy is usually reserved for patients who develop widespread cancer. It has been found that a premenopausal patient with widespread cancer may be helped by administration of testosterone (a male hormone). In contrast, a postmenopausal woman may be helped by the administration of estrogen (a female hormone).

Immunotherapy. A very new area of cancer treatment which is still in early research stages. Doctors hope some day to be able to cause the body to "reject" and destroy cancer the way it rejects and destroys bacteria or transplanted foreign tissue. So far, unfortunately, the results of experimental immunotherapy have been greatly inferior to those of surgery, radiation therapy, or chemotherapy.

Lymph. A clear fluid containing cells known as lymphocytes, which fight infection and also have a limited ability to fight cancer.

Lymph node. This is an organized mass of lymphocytes (see "lymph") that functions to "filter" the lymph fluid. The "kernels" or "glands" you feel in your neck when you have a bad sore throat are lymph nodes. Lymph nodes are important because cancer may lodge in them and grow there.

Lymphatics. Tiny vessels that carry lymph away from tissues to the lymph nodes. The lymph is ultimately returned to the bloodstream. The lymphatics also can carry cancer to the lymph nodes, the bloodsteam, and thus ultimately to the rest of the body.

Local anesthetic. A method of anesthesia or pain relief in which only the local area of concern is "put to sleep." This is usually done by injection a Novocain-like drug into the area. If you have had your teeth "put to sleep" for dental work, you know what a local anesthetic is like. A local anesthetic is less dangerous and less expensive than a general anesthetic. (See "general anesthetic")

Lumpectomy. The removal of a lump only. This is not regarded by most doctors as adequate treatment for cancer. At a minimum, most doctors think it should be followed by radiation therapy or chemotherapy.

Malignant. This means cancer.

Mammogram. A special X ray of the breast that can detect tumors before they can be felt. Usually they are taken from several angles in order to see all of the inside of the breast clearly. (See "xerogram")

Mammography. The process of making mammograms.

Menarche. The age at which a girl's menstrual period begins. For reasons that are not well understood, it occurs at different ages in different girls. Also poorly understood is the fact that the average age of menarche in the United States has lowered in the last seventy years.

Menopause. The menopause, often referred to as the change of life, is a cessation of menstrual function in a woman. It usually occurs between ages forty and fifty. At the time of menopause, the ovaries sharply decrease their production of estrogen.

Metastasis. The process by which a cancer spreads from where it originated (the primary tumor) to distant parts of the body. Tiny clumps of cells break off from the tumor and are carried in the lymphatic vessels and/or the bloodstream to a distant part of the body. An example of this is when breast cancer spreads to the liver. The new tumor in the liver is said to have "metastasized" to the liver and such a tumor is often referred to as a "metastatic" tumor.

Metastatic workup. The process by which physicians check the body for any indication of widespread cancer. This process should be initiated before any definitive cancer treatment is begun. Sadly, all too often this is not the case.

Modified radical mastectomy. In this operation the breast and lymph nodes in the axilla are removed. It represents a modification of the classical, or Halsted, radical mastectomy (see "radical mastectomy") because the large muscles of the front of the chest wall are not removed. This generally results in a better appearance of the chest wall and better function of the arm after surgery. Many surgeons are now adopting this operation for surgery for cancer of the breast.

Needle biopsy. In a needle biopsy, a hollow needle is inserted into the tumor and a core specimen is withdrawn. For breast biopsies, sometimes an adequate amount of tissue can be withdrawn and sometimes not. Also, there is the problem that the needle may miss the tumor if it is small and deep. This type of biopsy requires local anesthetic only.

Node. A shortened term doctors often use in place of "lymph node." (See "lymph node")

Oncologist. A doctor who spends a major part of his time either studying or treating cancer.

Oncology. The study of cancer.

One-stage treatment (one-stage procedure). In this scheme of treatment for breast cancer, a biopsy is performed under general anesthesia, and if cancer is found on a "frozen-section" examination (see "frozen section") of the tumor, the surgeon immediately does a mastectomy. The disadvantages of this treatment are obvious:

1. The three out of four women who will prove to have benign breast lumps will be subjected to the additional expense and danger of a general anesthetic.

2. Every woman undergoing breast biopsy in the one-stage treatment has to face the terrifying possibility that she will wake up without a breast.

3. There is not enough time for the pathologist to thoroughly study the tumor specimen, increasing the danger that an erroneous diagnosis of cancer could be made and a breast removed because of it. The tumor often cannot be fully evaluated by the pathologist.

4. Unless all necessary tests are done prior to the biopsy, the doctor has no time to try to determine by scan and X rays whether or not widespread disease is present. Doing the tests, including liver scans and bone scans, on every woman who has a biopsy will unnecessarily add greatly to the medical bills of the three out of four patients with benign disease who don't need these tests.

5. The one patient out of four who does have cancer may be subjected to an unnecessary radical mastectomy. The radical mastectomy is an operation designed to cure breast cancer. It will fail if there is already cancer elsewhere in the body. Time and again, patients have radical procedures performed on them when less extensive treatment, such as simple mastectomy, radiation therapy, or chemotherapy, would suffice.

6. The doctor does not have time to carefully plan the patient's treatment in accordance with every possible piece of data he can gather.

7. The patient has much less chance to participate in decisions about her own treatment. Those decisions, after all, affect *her* destiny—not the doctor's.

8. The patient has no time to prepare herself psychologically for her treatment.

9. The doctor is legally obliged to inform his biopsy patient about all the complications that could arise from a mastectomy. Since three out of four breast lumps will prove to be benign, he

has wasted his time with this discussion in three out of four patients. Despite all these drawbacks, many doctors cling to this approach, vehemently insisting that to delay surgery for even a day or two will lead to fatal spread of the disease. At this time modern medical literature substantially refutes this belief.

Oöphorectomy. The surgical removal of the ovaries. In breast cancer patients with widespread disease, this operation sometimes provides relief.

Partial mastectomy. Removal of a part of the breast. If it is done for cancer, a wide margin of tissue around the tumor and also the overlying skin is removed. Thus, this is a larger procedure than a lumpectomy. (See "lumpectomy") Most doctors do not consider partial mastectomy a good operation for cancer, since all the tumor may not be removed and the axilla is not explored to find out if there is cancer present. However, this operation is done and followed up with radiation therapy to help kill remaining cancer. It may be done in patients whose general medical condition prohibits more extensive surgery or in patients who absolutely refuse radical mastectomy or modified radical mastectomy.

Pectoralis muscles (pectoralis major and pectoralis minor). These are the two muscles on the front of the chest that support the breasts.

Primary tumor. The tumor at the place where the cancer began. It is called a primary tumor because it is the first tumor. In the instance of breast cancer, doctors may refer to the diseased breast as the "primary site." (Compare this with metastasis or a metastatic tumor.)

Progesterone. Another hormone in addition to estrogen that is important to a woman's physiology.

Radiation therapy. This is the use of high-voltage X rays many times more powerful than normal ones—powerful enough to kill cancer cells. Often used as a supplement to breast surgery. Radiation therapy can be used preoperatively or postoperatively.

Radical mastectomy. A very large operation in which the breast is removed along with the attached skin and nipple, the fat under the skin surrounding the breast, the pectoralis muscles (see "pectoralis muscles"), and all of the fat and lymph nodes that are contained in the axilla (armpit). The purpose of this operation is to remove all possible cancer near the primary site. This, or the modified radical mastectomy (see "modified radical mastectomy"), is the operation that most women in this country with cancer now receive. The idea that this is the best operation is now being increasingly questioned.

Scan. A process that can be used to outline an internal organ and to detect the presence of cancer or other diseases. There are several type of scans that may be needed for a breast cancer patient. These include liver scans, bone scans, and brain scans. They are made by injecting small amounts of weakly radioactive material into the patient's bloodstream and then measuring the radiation that is being given off by the organ being studied. The radioactive materials are chosen so that they are selectively absorbed by the organ to be studied and so that they decay to nonradioactive compounds fairly quickly. One important point about scans—they are helpful in the search for distant cancer. *Thus, at least liver and bone scans should be done prior to attempts at cure by surgery.* A woman who has detectable disease in the liver, bones, or other sites is not curable by surgery. Thus, she should not be subjected to aggressive operations such as the radical mastectomy until she has been thoroughly examined for widespread cancer by all means available. This leads to one of the central theses of this book—the need for two-stage treatment. If a surgeon makes the diagnosis of breast cancer and then immediately proceeds to do a radical mastectomy, there is no problem. There is obviously no time to do the tests needed by the "cancer" patient. It would be unwise and economically unjustifiable to subject each patient with a breast *lump* to these tests, since three out of four breast lumps are benign. However, if there is a few days' delay between biopsy and definitive treatment, there is time to perform the tests on the cancer patient. Another important point about scans—a "positive scan" can be caused by conditions other than cancer. Thus, a scan must be interpreted by the doctor in the context of the overall situation. Because of the fairly non-specific nature of scans, some skepticism is in order. Scans also must be performed by doctors and technicians who are thoroughly qualified.

Simple mastectomy. Removal of the breast and the skin and nipple of the breast. The axilla is not explored.

Thermography. This is a new largely experimental technique in which areas of the body, in this case the breasts, can be investigated by measuring the heat that is given off. A picture of this heat pattern is taken. Unfortunately, the results of this technique in terms of cancer detection thus far have been very disappointing.

Tumor. A mass or swelling. It can be benign or malignant.

Two-Stage Procedure. (See also one-stage procedure). This means that the process of treating a cancer is divided into two parts. First, a biopsy is performed (preferably under local anesthetic). Then there is a delay of a few days during which the biopsy tissue is carefully studied by the pathologist. If the diagnosis is cancer, the second stage is a complete evaluation of the patient, using tests and scans to see if the cancer has spread beyond the breast and into the body. The type of treatment instituted depends on the decision of the doctor and the patient in reviewing the overall situation.

The belief that delay between biopsy and cancer treatment will lessen the patient's chance of survival is not supported by current medical literature.

Sources

Cancer Staging

T.N.M. Classification of Tumors, International Meeting Against Cancer. Geneva, Switzerland, 1973.

Cancer Statistics 1974

Worldwide Epidemiology. New York: American Cancer Society (Professional Education Publication).

General Comprehensive Information

HAAGENSEN, C. D., *Diseases of the Breast.* 2nd ed. Philadelphia: Saunders, 1972.

Implications of Delay in Cancer

CLEARY, H. P., Correspondence. *New England Journal of Medicine* 811 (October 11, 1973), 289.

FEINSTEIN, A. R., "The Epidemiology of Cancer *Therapy.*" *Archives Internal Medicine* 123 (1969), 171–86.

"Everything You Did Not Want to Know About the Patient But Were Afraid to Ask." *Journal of the American Medical Society* 225 (1973), 165.

Jane Cowles

FEINSTEIN, A. R., "A New Staging System for Cancer and a Reappraisal of 'Early' Treatment and 'Cure' by Radical Surgery." *New England Journal of Medicine* 279 (1968), 747–53.
HACKETT, T. P., N. H. CASSEN, and J. W. RAKER, "Patient Delay in Cancer." *New England Journal of Medicine* 289 (1973), 1473.

Inadequacies of Breast Examination by Physicians

DAY, E., BENNETT, and L. VENET. "Periodic Cancer Detection Examinations as a Cancer Control Measure." *Fourth National Cancer Conference Proceedings*, Philadelphia: Lippincott (1961), 705–7.
GERSHON-COHEN, J., B. HERMAN, and S. M. BERGER. "Detection of Breast Cancer by Periodic X-Ray Examination." *Journal of the American Medical Association* 176 (1961), 1114–16.
GILBERSSEN, V. A., "Survival of Asymptomatic Breast Cancer Patients." *Surgery, Gynecology and Obstetrics* 122 (1966) 81–83.
HAAGENSEN, C. D., *Diseases of the Breast.* 2nd ed. Philadelphia: Saunders, 1972.
HOLLED, A. I., L. VENET, E. DAY, and S. HOYT, "Breast Cancer Detection by Routine Physical Examinations." *New York Journal of Medicine* 60 (1960), 832–27.
HUTCHINSON, G. B., and S. SHAPIRO, "Lead Time Gained by Diagnostic Screening for Breast Cancer." *Journal of the National Cancer Institute* 41 (1968), 665–81.
SHAPIRO, S., P. STRAX, and L. VENET, "Periodic Breast Cancer Screening in Reducing Fatality for Breast Cancer." *Journal of the American Medical Association* 215 (1971), 1777–85.
STRAX, P., L. VENET, and S. SHAPIRO, "Mass Screening in Mammary Cancer." *Cancer* 23 (1969), 875–18.
URBAN, J. A., "Treatment of Early Cancer in the Breast." *Postgraduate Medicine* 27 (1970), 389–93.

The Psychological Aspects of Life-Threatening Diseases

KUBLER-ROSS, E., *On Death and Dying.* New York: Macmillan, 1969.
SCOTT-MAXWELL, F., *The Measure of My Days.* New York: Knopf, 1968.
TROEBST, C. C., *The Art of Survival.* New York: Doubleday, 1965.

Modes of Treatment—Surgery, Chemotherapy, Hormone Therapy, Radiation Therapy: General Information

ATKINS, H., "The Treatment of Breast Cancer." *Social Medicine* 67 (April, 1974), 277–86.

CARBONE, P. P., "Cancer Teaching Symposium on Breast Cancer: A Challenging Problem." *Recent Results Cancer* 42 (1973), 144–50

DEL REGATO, J. and J. ACKERMAN, *Cancer Diagnosis, Treatment and Prognosis.* 4th ed. St. Louis: Mosby, 1973.

FLETCHER, G. H., *Textbook of Radiotherapy.* 2nd ed. Philadelphia: Lea & Febiger, 1973.

GREENWALD, E. S., *Cancer Chemotherapy.* 2nd ed. Flushing, New York: Medical Examination Publishing Company, 1973.

HAAGENSEN, C. D., *Diseases of the Breast.* 2nd ed. Philadelphia: Saunders, 1972.

Outpatient Breast Biopsy

ABRAMSON, D. J., "850–7 Biopsies as an Out-Patient Procedure: Delayed Mastectomy in 41 Cases." *Annals of Surgery* 163 (1966), 478–83.

CRILE, G., JR., *et al.*, "A New Look at Biopsy of the Breast." *American Journal of Surgery* 126 (1973), 117–19.

GOLDMAN, W. P., "Triple Biopsy for Carcinoma of the Breast. A Clinical Study of 200 Cases." *Surgery* 70 (1971), 628–34.

JACKSON, P. P., and H. H. PITTS, "Biopsy with Delayed Radical Mastectomy for Carcinoma of the Breast." *American Journal of Surgery* 98 (1969), 184–89.

SALTZSTEIN, E. C., *et al.*, "Ambulatory Surgical Units: An Alternative to Hospitalization." *Archives of Surgery* 108 (1974), 143–46.

SCOTT, A., "Delayed Operation for Breast Carcinoma." *Surgery, Gynecology and Obstetrics* 131 (1970), 291.

SKARLOFF, D. N., and N. D. CHARLES, "Bone Metastases from Breast Cancer at the Time of Radical Mastectomy." *Surgery, Gynecology and Obstetrics* 127 (1968), 763–68.

Pathology

Cancer: A Manual for Practitioners. 4th ed. American Cancer Society, New York: 1968.

FOULDS, L., *Neoplastic Development.* Vol. I. London and New York: Academic Press, 1969.

"Standardized Management of Breast Specimens." *American Journal of Clinical Pathology.* Vol. 60, No. 6 (December, 1973).

TERRY, R., *What the Medical Oncologist Needs to Know About Histopathology.* USC in-hospital article, 1974. Los Angeles County General Hospital, Los Angeles, California.

VAN DER REIS, L., *The Wayward Cell: CA: Its Origins, Nature, and Treatment.* 1st ed. Berkeley, California: University of California Press, 1972.

Plastic and Reconstructive Surgery

JENNY, H., "A More Humane Approach to the Problem of Breast Cancer." Paper presented to the Plastic and Reconstructive Society, San Francisco, 1974.

LEWIS, J. R., JR., "Reconstruction of the Breast." *Journal of American Surgery* 51/2 (1971), 429–39.

MLADICJ, R. D., JR., "Breast Reconstruction After Surgery and Trauma," F. W. Masters and J. R. Lewis, Jr., eds. *Symposium on Esthetic Surgery of the Face, Eyelid and Breast,* (1972), 209–15.

SNYDERMAN, R. K., and R. H. GUTHRIE, "Reconstruction of the Female Breast Following Radical Mastectomy." *Journal of Plastic and Reconstructive Surgery* 47 (1961), 565–67.

Psychological Aspects: A Review of Recent Literature

AKERHERST, A. C., "Post-Mastectomy Morale." *Lancet* 2 (1972), 181–82.

ANSTICE, E., "The Emotional Operation. *Nursing Times* 66 (1970), 837–38.

BRANDON, S., "Crisis Theory and Possibilities of Therapeutic Intervention." *British Journal of Psychiatry* 117 (1970), 627–33.

CAPLEN, G., ed., *Cancer Facts and Figures.* New York: American Cancer Society, 1971. *Prevention of Mental Disorders.* New York: Basic Books, 1969.

Guidelines for Cancer Care. Committee on Guidelines for Cancer Care. Chicago: American College of Surgeons, 1971.

HEALEY, J. E., ed., *Ecology of the Cancer Patient*. Washington, D.C.: Interdisciplinary Associates, 1970.

Proceedings: Symposium on Rehabilitation in Cancer. New York: American Cancer Society, 1969.

JANIS, I., *Psychological Stress*. New York: John Wiley, 1958.

TRACHTENBERG, J. M., "Team Involvement in the Problems Incurred." Presented at the Fifteenth Annual Clinical Conference on Progress of the Cancer Patient, N. D. Anderson Hospital, Austin, Texas, 1970.

URBAN, J. A., "Psychological Aspects of Radical Mastectomy Immediately After Biopsy." *Journal of the American Medical Association* 230, No. 1 (October 7, 1974).

Rehabilitation Medicine in Breast Cancer

BYRD, B. F. "Rehabilitation of the Patient with Breast Cancer." *Seventh National Cancer Conference Proceedings. September 28-29, 1972*. Philadelphia: Lippincott, 1972.

LASSER, T., *A Manual for Women Who Have Had Breast Surgery*. 2nd ed. New York: American Cancer Society, 1972.

MAYO, DUDLEY, "Contributions of Pure Science to Progressive Medicine." *Journal of the American Medical Association* 84 (1965), 1465–69.

The Rights of Patients

ANNAS, G. J., *The Rights of Hospital Patients*. New York: Discus Books/Avon, 1975.

GAYLIN, R., "The Patient's Bill of Rights." *Saturday Review of Science* (March, 1973).

HOLDER, A., "Informed (but Uneducated) Consent." *New England AMA*, 1970.

INGELFINGER, "Informed (but Uneducated) Consent." *New England Journal of Medicine* 287 (1972), 465–66.

The Institutional Guide to MHEW Policy on Protection of Human Subjects. HEW, Washington, D.C., 1975.

McCARTHY and WIDMER, "Effects of Screening by Consultants on Recommended Elective Surgical Procedures." *New England Journal of Medicine* 291 (1974), 1331–35.

Further Reading

General

AKEHURST, A. D., "Post-Mastectomy Morale." *Lancet* 2 (1972), 181–82.

AQUILERA, D. C., J. M. MESSICK, and M. S. FARRELL, *Crisis Intervention; Theory in Methodology*. St. Louis: Mosby, 1970.

BARCKLEY, V., "Grief, A Part of Living." *Ohio's Health* 20 (1968), 34–38.

CRARY, W. G., and C. W. JOHNSON, "Attitude Therapy in a Crisis Intervention Program. *Hospital Community Psychiatry* 21 (1970), 165–68.

EARLE, A. S., "Delayed Operation for Breast Carcinoma." *Surgery, Gynecology and Obstetrics* 291 (August, 1970).

EGBERT, L. D., G. E. BATTIT, H. TURNDORF, and H. K. BEECHER, "The Value of the Preoperative Visit by an Anesthetist." *Journal of the American Medical Association* 185 (1963), 533–55.

ENELOW, and WEXLER, M., *Psychiatry in the Practice of Medicine*. New York: Oxford University Press, 1966.

ERVIN, C. J., *The Psychological Adjustment to Mastectomy*.

FRANCES, V., B. M. KORSCH, and N. J. MORRIS, "Gaps in Doctor-Patient Relationship." *New England Journal of Medicine* 280 (1969), 535–40.

GALLUP, G., "Women's Attitudes Regarding Breast Cancer." *Consumer Reports* (March, 1974).

HALL, T., "The General Management of the Patient with Advanced Cancer." *Journal of the St. Barnabas Medical Center* 7 (1970), 51–57.

KUBLER-ROSS, E., "What Is It Like to be Dying?" *American Journal of Nursing* 71 (1971), 54–60.

LASSER, T., *A Manual for Women Who Have Had Breast Surgery.* New York: American Cancer Society, 1969.

OKEN, D., "What to Tell Cancer Patients," *Journal of the American Medical Association* 1975: 86–94, 1961.

PADILLA, G., "Second Quarterly Project Report to the American Cancer Society of California," 1973.

PECK, A., "Emotional Reactions to Having Cancer." *American Journal of Roentgen, Radium Therapy and Nuclear Medicine* 114 (1972), 591–99.

REESE, E. P., *The Analysis of Human Behavior.* Dubuque, Iowa: William C. Brown, 1966.

Rehabilitation of the Breast Patient. New York: American Cancer Society, 1972.

SCHWARTZ, S. I., *Principles of Surgery* ("The Effects of Anesthesia"). New York: McGraw-Hill, 1974.

Breast Self-Examination

Breast Self-Examination. New York: American Cancer Society, 1975.

CUTLER, MAX. Paper Presented to the UCLA Reconstruction Seminar, Los Angeles, California, May, 1975. Also personal communication.

High-Risk Category. New York: American Cancer Society, 1975.

Mammography and Xerography

DOOLEY, R., J. WOLFE, and HARKINS, "Xeroradiography of the Breast: A Comparative Study with Conventional Film Mammography." *Cancer* 28 (December, 1971), 1569–74.

GERSHON-COHEN, J., and H. INGLEBY, "Carcinoma of the Breast: Roentgenographic Technique and Diagnostic Criteria." *Radiology* 60 (1952), 68–76.

SILVERSTEIN, M. J. Personal communication.

Informed Consent

STEVENS, G. M., and J. F. EWIGEN, "Mammography Survey for Breast Cancer Detection. A Two-Year Study of 1223 Clinically Negative Asymptomatic Women over Forty." *Cancer* 19 (1966), 51–59.

STARKS, P., L. VENET, and S. SHAPIRO, "Value of Mammography in Reduction of Mortality from Breast Cancer in Mass Screening." *American Journal of Roentgenology* 117 (March, 1973), 688–89.

WILKENSON, E. Personal communication, 1974.

WOLFE, J. N., *Xeroradiography*. Springfield, Illinois: Charles C. Thomas, 1972.

For a complete doctor's information package regarding the advantages and reprints of xeroradiography, have your doctor send a note to the Xerox Corporation, Xeroradiography Department, 125 North Vinedo Street, PO Box 5786, Pasadena, California 91107.

Outpatient Biopsy

ABRAMSON, D. J., "857 Breast Biopsies as an Outpatient Procedure: Delayed Mastectomy in 41 Malignant Cases." *American Surgeon* 163 (1966), 479–83. Abramson summarizes the following important observations:

"From 1950 through December, 1962, biopsies of lesions of the breast considered clinically benign were performed under local anesthesia in the outpatient department of the Walter Reed Army Medical Center, Washington, D.C.

"This is the largest of such series reported.

"Outpatient management had saved hospital beds, eased operating schedules, and saved expensive and costly diagnostic study and preparation. In patients with benign lesions the psychological advantage is obvious since the procedure is minor and the patient can go home after the frozen section is reported negative. In patients with malignant lesions, there is always psychological trauma.

"The five-year survival of patients with malignant lesions was determined. . . . The five-year survival was 78.4 percent (evidence that there was no deleterious effect on surival when radical mastectomy was delayed during this time interval)."

CAFFEE, J., and R. BENFIELD, "Data Favoring Biopsy of the Breast

Jane Cowles

Under Local Anesthesia." *Surgery, Gynecology and Obstetrics* 140 (1975), 88–90. Summary:

"Experience with 184 consecutive biopsies of the breast, 447 benign lesions, and 37 carcinomas over an 18-month period has been reviewed. Local anesthesia was used in 78 percent of the patients, and it was the method of choice whenever the preoperative diagnosis was benign. General anesthesia was used when a lesion was thought likely to be malignant. Anesthesia within these guidelines was used in 88 percent of the patients with correct preoperative diagnosis. Exceptions were made primarily but not exclusively, because of the patients' preference.

"The preoperative diagnoses were correct in 168 patients, unstated in five, and incorrect in 11. Six women were originally thought to have carcinoma, and five women unexpectedly had malignant disease."

Cowles, J. K. Personal observation. Summary:

"Patients at Los Angeles County General Hospital have routinely received biopsies using the local anesthetic method for the last five years. It was my personal observation, from September, 1974, to April, 1975, that the majority of women undergoing this procedure tolerated it extremely well, particularly after being the beneficiaries of patient discussion groups before the biopsies. This form of biopsy was generally used for all patients with breast masses. The rate of benign tumors fell into the national limits of 75 to 78 percent. Biopsies were performed twice a week. The highest number reaching 14 in one day, to the possible lowest number of 5 on the following day. Patients were discharged on the afternoon following a morning biopsy, unless otherwise indicated.

"The Los Angeles County General Hospital attempted, in cases where a diagnosis of breast cancer had been made, to complete a thorough metastatic evaluation of each patient before *any* definitive treatment was begun. The results served as indication for whether any widespread cancer was present, and also as a baseline study for future comparisons."

Crile, G., Jr., *et al.*, "A New Look at Biopsy of the Breast." *American Journal of Surgery* 126 (1973), 117–19, In this article Dr. Crile summarizes the following important observations concerning breast biopsies:

"There have been several excellent studies showing that a delay of a few days between biopsy and definitive treatment has no adverse effect on survival. In fact, most of the studies suggest that the results are better after delay, either because of the selection of cases, or because there is some advantage in removing a primary tumor sometime before dissecting a regional node. In any event, there appears to be no support for the widespread belief that it is necessary to perform a definitive operation immediately after biopsy."

EARLE, A. S., "Delayed Operation for Breast Carcinoma." *Surgery, Gynecology and Obstetrics* 291 (August, 1970). The following editorial by Earle illustrates his findings:

"There are few procedures that are so stereotyped that they do not deserve an occasional reevaluation, including even the time-honored approach to the surgical treatment of carcinoma of the breast.

"Contrary to common belief, immediate mastectomy after a positive biopsy does not insure a higher survival rate. There is now a convincing accumulation of evidence to show that a delay of a few days between the time of the biopsy and the mastectomy is not harmful.

"A delay of several days can be used advantageously for the remaining ten percent or so of the women with proved malignant lesions. First and of greatest importance, is that disseminated disease can be ruled out as far as possible."

GOLDMAN, W. P., "Triple Biopsy for Carcinoma of the Breast: A Clinical Study of 200 Cases," *Surgeon* 70 (1971), 628–33. Summary:

"Delays as long as fourteen days between preliminary biopsy and final radical mastectomy have not had deleterious effects on survival rates. (Again, a short delay is safe.)"

JACKSON, P., and H. PITTS, "Biopsy with Delayed Radical Mastectomy for Carcinoma of the Breast." *American Journal of Surgery* 98 (1959), 184–89.

This article is of extreme interest, for it goes into a thorough review of the literature, which notes that there seems to be no problem regarding the survival rate of those patients who underwent immediate surgery and those patients who had a delay of surgery between biopsy of the breast and surgery. Summary:

"In this small series of cases in which 51 biopsy specimens were received, a mastectomy was performed on the average of 18.4 days later, and we have shown on an overall survival rate of 62.7 percent of five-year cures."

PEACOCK, E. E., "Yet Another Form of Women's Liberation." *American Journal of Surgery* 124 (1972), 565–67. This editorial succinctly addresses itself to some broader principles of a different approach to biopsy and treatment of breast disease.

"Prior to 1960, women seldom questioned the surgeon on the advisability to treating lumps in the breast by hospitalization, biopsy under general anesthesia, and radical mastectomy if a lesion was malignant. . . . The difference in patients' attitudes now as compared to fourteen years ago is striking. Although patients seldom express such thoughts directly to surgeons, I believe that many women in 1972 simply are not willing to have a decision about treatment of breast cancer made while they are anesthestized. . . . Many intelligent women wish to participate in the development of a treatment plan. Moreover, they do not want to participate in making such decisions while lying in a supine position, in the unfamiliar surroundings of an operating room, and outnumbered by relative strangers. Unfortunately, however, many patients who are not willing to have decisions made under these circumstances express their unwillingness by going to another surgeon."

SALTZSTEIN, E. C., *et al.*, "Ambulatory Surgical Unit Alternative to Hospitalization." *Archives of Surgery* 108 (1974), 143–45. Saltzstein came to the following conclusion in his article:

"A fifteen-month experience with an ambulatory surgical unit has been presented. High-quality medical care has been rendered to patients undergoing surgical procedures as out-patients, while inpatient bed utilization and hospitalization costs were dramatically reduced. An ambulatory surgical unit is a viable alternative to inpatient hospitalization.

"In interests of good quality medical care, and in interests of controlling spiraling medical costs, we believe the patient, physician, hospital, and the third-party payor should insist on the performance of surgical procedures on an outpatient basis when feasible.

"It is also noted in this article that the average length of stay for the breast biopsy patient on an inpatient basis is 2.4 days as compared to 4.3 hours on an outpatient basis. The total mean cost is the difference between $415 for inpatients and $200 for outpatients . . .

not including surgical fees. He notes that hospital charges range from 47 percent to 70 percent higher for inpatients as for outpatients undergoing similar procedures. Screening tests and room charges to inpatients accounted for the significant cost spiral. This demonstrates that out-patient breast biopsy is cheaper, and consumes less of the patient's time."

SKLAROFF, D. N., and CHARKES, "Bone Metastasis from Breast Cancer," *Surgery, Gynecology and Obstetrics* 763 (1968), 768. This study says in effect that about 3,200 women would undergo needless radical mastectomy in 1968: "The importance of adequately studying the patient for distant metastasis prior to definitive treatment is emphasized for observations such as these."

Additional Reading

ACHINCLOSE, H., JR., "Significance of Location and Number of Axillary Metastases, in Carcinoma of the Breast: A Justification for a Conservative Operation." *Annals of Surgery* 158 (1963), 37.

BRINKLEY, D., and J. BITTLE, "Treatment of Stage II Carcinoma of the Female Breast." *Lancet* 2 (1966), 291.

CRILE, G., JR., "Results of Simplified Treatment of Breast Cancer." *Surgery, Gynecology and Obstetrics* 132 (1971), 780.

PETERS, N. V., "Carcinoma of the Breast, Stage 2—Radiation Range; Wedge Resection and Irradiation: An Effective Treatment in Early Breast Cancer." *Journal of the American Medical Association* 200 (1967), 134.

WISE, L., A. Y. MASON, and L. ACKERMAN, "Local Excision and Irradiation; an Alternative Method for the Treatment of Early Breast Cancer." *Annals of Surgery* 174 (1971), 392.

The Breast Cancer Problem

ACKERMAN, L. V., and J. A. REGATO, *Cancer Diagnosis, Treatment and Prognosis.* 4th ed. St. Louis: Mosby. A respected book from which I have taken the scheme for classifying breast cancer.

BLOOM, H. J. G., "The Natural History of Untreated Breast Cancer." *Annals of Internal Medicine* 114 (1964), 747.

CONN, H. F., ed., *Current Therapy—1974.* Philadelphia: Saunders, 1974.

HAAGENSEN, C. D., *Diseases of the Breast.* 2nd ed. Philadelphia: Saunders, 1971. An excellent book from which I have drawn heavily.

HAMILTON, W. J., and H. W. MOSSMAN, *Human Embryology.* 4th ed. Baltimore: Williams & Wilkins, 1972.

HAMM, A. W., *Histology.* 5th ed. Philadelphia: Lippincott, 1965.

KUSAMA, S., et al., *The Gross Rates of Growth of Human Mammary Carcinoma.* Cancer Volume 30, 1972.

OCHNER, A., "Diseases of the Breast." *Postgraduate Medicine* 57, No. 3, 1975.

ROBBINS, S. L., *Pathology.* 3rd ed. Philadelphia: Saunders, 1968. One of the more popular standard pathology texts.

RUBIN, P., ed., *Clinical Oncology for Medical Students and Physicians, A Multidisciplinary Approach.* 3rd ed. Rochester: American Cancer Society, 1970–71. An excellent overview of the cancer field for doctors.

Jane Cowles

SCHWARTZ, S. I., ed., *Principals of Surgery*. New York. McGraw-Hill, 1974.

SILVERBERG, E., and A. HOLLEB, "Cancer Statistics, 1974—World Wide Epidemiology." *CA—A Cancer Journal for Clinicians* 24 (1974). From which I took my data on factors that raise or lower a woman's risk of breast cancer.

————, "Cancer Statistics, 1976: A Comparison of White and Black Populations." *CA—A Cancer Journal for Clinicians* 26 (1976).

INDEX